D1426484

0008005303

**Books are to be returned on or before
the last date below**

# EASTERN AND
# WESTERN
# EUROPE
## IN THE MIDDLE AGES

Edited with an introduction by
GEOFFREY BARRACLOUGH

# EASTERN AND WESTERN EUROPE
## IN THE MIDDLE AGES

F. GRAUS   K. BOSL   F. SEIBT
M. M. POSTAN   A. GIEYSZTOR

with 132 illustrations, 16 in colour

THAMES AND HUDSON · LONDON

*The chapters by Professors Graus and Seibt were translated from the German by Marion Jackson and the chapter by Professor Gieysztor was translated from the French by Heather Karolyi.*

*Printed and bound in Great Britain by Jarrold and Sons Ltd Norwich*

*0 500 32018 7 clothbound*

*0 500 33018 2 paperbound*

# CONTENTS

INTRODUCTION: TOWARDS A NEW
CONCEPT OF EUROPEAN HISTORY
*Geoffrey Barraclough*                                    7

I    SLAVS AND GERMANS
     *Frantisek Graus*                                   15

II   POLITICAL RELATIONS BETWEEN
     EAST AND WEST
     *Karl Bosl*                                         43

III  THE RELIGIOUS PROBLEMS
     *Ferdinand Seibt*                                   83

IV   ECONOMIC RELATIONS BETWEEN
     EASTERN AND WESTERN EUROPE
     *M. M. Postan*                                     125

V    CULTURAL INTERCHANGES
     *Alexander Gieysztor*                              175

     BIBLIOGRAPHICAL NOTES                              207

     SOURCES OF ILLUSTRATIONS                           211

     INDEX                                              212

1 Cameo commemorating Germanicus' triumphal reception in Rome after his defeat of the German tribes in A D 14. Centre, the general stands before the emperor Tiberius; above, the 'divine' Germanicus, mounted on Pegasus, is welcomed into Olympus.

# INTRODUCTION: TOWARDS A NEW CONCEPT OF EUROPEAN HISTORY

*Geoffrey Barraclough*

This volume represents, in intention at least, a foray into a new field of history. Down to 1945 – in many popular accounts even after 1945 – the history of eastern and western Europe and of their relations through the ages was portrayed as a grim story of racial struggle, a relentless conflict of Teutons and Slavs, or even as an ineluctable clash of civilizations. Germans came to see themselves as the defenders of European civilization against the Slav masses of the East. Poles and Czechs retorted by denouncing the German *Drang nach Osten*, accusing the Germans of ten centuries of 'aggressive expansion' aimed at 'the conquest, subjugation and exploitation' of the Slav territories lying beyond their eastern frontiers.

If it is true, as is often said, that every generation must reinterpret its past and write its own history in the light of its own experience, it is obvious that this traditional interpretation will no longer do. For one thing, it reflects, and projects back into the Middle Ages, the national antagonisms of the second half of the nineteenth and the first half of the twentieth centuries; it is far less an expression of dispassionate historical research than of the passions aroused by Pan-Slavism and Pan-Germanism, and of the 'social Darwinism' which was so powerful an influence in late nineteenth-century thought. And, secondly, it reflects a conception of European history which has been overtaken by events. For Leopold von Ranke, who first expressed this conception in outline in 1824, European history was in all essential ways 'western' history; the 'Romano-Germanic peoples' of western Europe formed 'a world for themselves', in which the peoples of eastern Europe participated not at all, or at best as silent spectators. Thus Europe was divided into two historical areas – a western area populated by Germans and

Latins, and an eastern area identified with the Slavs – and all the emphasis fell on the western half. The Romano-Germanic world was, in Ranke's words, the foundation upon which 'the whole development of our condition down to the most recent times has depended'.

It would be absurd to claim that this view of European history is extinct. It was perpetuated by Arnold Toynbee who, taking over Ranke's categories, claimed to see in 'western society' an 'intelligible field of study' distinct and separate from what he called the 'Orthodox Christian civilization' of eastern Europe. It is enshrined – surprisingly, perhaps, in view of the large east European ingredient in the population of the United States – in American university education, which places great emphasis on teaching the formation of 'western civilization'. And yet, as an interpretation of European history, Ranke's scheme reflects only too clearly a particular situation which has long since passed away. In 1824, when eastern Europe was either partitioned between Prussia, Austria and Russia or submerged under Turkish rule, Ranke's point of view was perhaps comprehensible. Today, it is evidently in need of revision. With a new balance in Europe between East and West, and a new balance between Europe and the extra-European world, there is an urgent need for a new, less one-sided approach to European history than the one we have inherited. The origins of the east European peoples, the cross-currents running between them and the peoples of the West, the sources and character of their ideas and attitudes – all questions carrying us back to what we call the Middle Ages – are essential knowledge in the world in which we live.

It is as a contribution to this overdue revision that the present volume has been written. As Karl Bosl emphasizes (below, p. 82), the Slav nations of eastern Europe are constituent elements of European civilization just as much as the Romano-Germanic nations of the West; and the main purpose of the following pages is to show something of the process by which they 'became fully fledged members of the Christian society of

8

medieval Europe'. The idea of a ceaseless conflict between Germans and Slavs is not borne out by an objective study of the historical evidence; indeed, the very conceptions 'German' and 'Slav', as Frantisek Graus demonstrates, are scholarly constructions, which hide the diversity of the many tribes and peoples inhabiting this area; and nothing is clearer than that linguistic affinities were rarely conducive to national or political identity. German tribe fought German tribe, Slav tribe fought Slav tribe, as much and with as great impunity as Slav fought German. But by the same token Slavs and Germans co-operated across a fluctuating and uncertain frontier, and the significant process, throughout the medieval centuries, is cultural and racial assimilation, rather than strife. We must never forget that appellations like 'German' and 'Slav' are descriptive of language and culture, not of race. The peoples of Europe are mixtures of basic racial types, found in varying proportions over the whole continent; their assembly into 'nations' – Poles, Czechs, Prussians, Bavarians, and the like – is a consequence of a long process of historical development in different environments. The nation, in short, is a result, and not a precondition, of historical development; and we shall get our whole picture of European history wrong if, even unconsciously, we assume the opposite.

This development, in essentials, took place in the Middle Ages; and this is one reason why the medieval background is so important. By the fifteenth century the nations which would play a historic role in Europe's future were in existence, and the stage was set. But there is a second reason why the medieval centuries are important, for at the very time when the division into nations was taking place, the basis of a common civilization was being laid, in which all the peoples of Europe were called upon to participate. Ranke was not perhaps so far wrong when he spoke of European civilization as a 'unity in diversity'; his mistake was to confine this unity to western Europe. In reality, the early history of Europe was, in Graus's phrase, 'a melting-pot', out of which states with distinct traditions eventually arose, but all, as a result of long contact and interaction, sharing a common inheritance.

This book tries to show how, as a result of political and cultural interchange, of trading links and, perhaps above all, of participation in a common religious experience, a single civilization embracing both East and West (and, for the matter of that, both North and South) came into existence. It is concerned, therefore, more with co-operation than with conflict, with a process of assimilation rather than one of mutual repulsion and aversion; and in this process, as Ferdinand Seibt's contribution makes clear, the spread of Christianity played a central part. Religion is often treated as the most intractable wedge separating East and West; the breach between Greek Orthodoxy and Roman Catholicism is said to have been the factor heightening existing differences and making them irreconcilable. This may be true of Russia, which took its Christianity from Byzantium; it is not true of the borderlands lying between Russia and Germany. The impact of Greek Christianity, particularly of the famous mission of St Cyril and St Methodius, is discussed at a number of points in the pages which follow. Here it is sufficient to say that, while religion certainly drove a wedge between the south Slavs of Serbia and Bulgaria and the west Slavs north of the Carpathians – a wedge, however, which had already been established when the Hungarians took control in the intervening zone – and while it was later a source of friction between Poland and Muscovy, the impact of Greek Orthodoxy elsewhere was spasmodic and short-lived. Western influence, as Gieysztor says (p. 184), 'proved far more dynamic than Byzantine civilization and its derivatives'; and the church was the most active agent of cultural assimilation. 'Acceptance of the Christian faith', in Karl Bosl's words (p. 57), 'made the Slavs a part of the growing society of Europe.' At the same time it played a major part in the constitution of the Slavic states, assisting the centralizing efforts of the Přemyslid, Piast and Arpad dynasties, and helping them to resist the pressures of German expansion; indeed, at more than one critical juncture, it was the church and the bishops who stood out as the 'champions of national unity'.

No one, of course, would seek to deny or minimize the existence of conflict, particularly along what today are the borders of Germany and Poland. No phase of East-West relations in the Middle Ages is better known than the long series of wars between Poland and the Teutonic knights in Prussia, culminating in the battle of Tannenberg in 1410. But even earlier political relations between the nascent states were often the reverse of friendly; particularly in the reign of Henry II of Germany (1002–24) – often regarded (perhaps with some exaggeration) as the moment when a permanent 'gulf' was opened between East and West – German relations with Poland deteriorated drastically. But even this was not a racial conflict. Henry II, as Seibt points out (pp. 93–4), had no hesitation in allying with the heathen Liutizi, one of the Slav peoples on the Elbe, against the Polish king; and the Liutizi, the original inhabitants of the modern march of Lausitz, were willing to fight on Henry's side, because their independence and that of the other small Slav peoples along the Elbe was threatened, as much by Polish as by German expansion.

These were clashes of predatory expanding states, no different from similar clashes in the West, not part of an age-old contest of Slav and German. Rivalry and conflict between Poles and Czechs was as bitter and as frequent as rivalry between Poles and Germans; and if the Poles made every effort to conquer and absorb the small Slav tribes of the Elbe, it must be remembered also that it was a Polish duke who, in 1226, called in the German Order to help him conquer the heathen Prussians. The central theme of this book, however, is that war and conquest, though a constant accompaniment – almost a running commentary – is not the essence of the story, and must not be treated as such. Far more significant was the leavening process of attrition resulting from continuous, almost daily contact, the interaction at every level from the field to the castle and the church, through which differences of origin were gradually evened out, the 'pressure' (to quote Alexander Gieysztor) 'towards a uniform style of life' and 'the opportunities for intellectual exchange', which were 'an unfailing source of cultural enrichment.' The dominant feature, says Gieysztor (pp. 198–9), was not a 'collision of civilizations' but the emergence of a common civilization; and where there were conflicts, 'it was much more class than national or ethnic affiliations which accounted for common psychological reactions in the face of certain acute problems.'

Nor, without denying their predominance, should too much emphasis be placed on German-Slav relations. They were not the only point of contact. In the fourteenth century the Bohemian court had connections with France, the Hungarian court with Italy. The trading links of eastern Europe – particularly the great timber- and grain-exporting industries – extended far to the west, to England and Flanders, and the return cargoes included wine from Burgundy and Gascony, metal goods from Liège, leather and tin from England, and fish from Sweden; and even if, as Professor Postan argues (p. 174), long-distance trade – contrary to a commonly held belief – was ultimately a factor widening, rather than levelling out, the differences between eastern and western Europe, this does not detract from its significance in the first instance. For trading contacts brought other contacts in their wake, and as early as the tenth century the princely rulers of eastern Europe, seeking to 'create supra-tribal links, with the help of foreign models', began to send out to Liège, the 'Athens of the North', to Regensburg, to the cities of the Rhineland and to Rome for 'instructors in civilization', like Tuni, the Italian abbot, to whom Gieysztor refers (p. 180), or the canons, mentioned by Ferdinand Seibt (p. 112), who were called from Pavia to Raudnitz in Bohemia in 1333. The most graphic evidence of this cultural interchange, as the illustrations in this book so clearly demonstrate, is found in architecture, in the great brick churches and civic buildings which are found with no significant variation of style across the great northern plain from Lübeck to Toruń and as far as Riga, and the magnificent stone cathedrals and Cistercian abbeys inspired by French and Italian models, in the mountainous country further south. Finally, in the reign of Matthias Corvinus of Hungary (1458–90), the first breezes of the Florentine Renaissance, later to reach Cracow and Moscow, ruffled the skies of eastern Europe.

Certainly no one would suggest that the impact of this Christian civilization was uniform. The east European states were 'frontier' states – they saw themselves, as the Hungarians proudly announced around 1400, as 'the frontier guards of Christianity' – and in such a frontier environment their structure was inevitably different from that of the less exposed West. Moreover, the East, which (some Balkan regions apart) had never undergone the levelling process of Roman rule, and, unlike the Franks, had no Roman inheritance to aid it in its 'take-off', was slower to make a start. The mere fact that Cluniac monasticism only slowly penetrated the countries beyond the Elbe meant, as Seibt points out (p. 100), that 'The spirit of Cluniac reform made no headway in eastern Europe.' These are differentiating features, which it would be foolish to ignore. The important thing is that the time-lag (which can easily be exaggerated) was made up. By the end of the first millennium the Slavonic East had become an integral part of the European world; by the time of Casimir the Great of Poland (1333–70), Louis the Great of Hungary (1342–82) and Charles the Great of Bohemia (1333–78), the lands north of the Carpathians and east of the Elbe had entered the mainstream of European history, with a place of their own in the international economy.

Though no book dealing with eastern Europe in the Middle Ages can afford to ignore Kiev, Novgorod and Muscovy, this volume is more specifically concerned with the lands lying between Germany and Russia, the region between the Elbe and the Pripet marshes which Oskar Halecki called 'the borderlands of western civilization'. It is the work of five distinguished scholars, of whom one (Professor Postan) is English, one (Professor Gieysztor) is Polish, one (Professor Graus) is Czech, and two (Professor Bosl and Dr Seibt) are German. It draws on the best of recent historical scholarship from both sides of the current political demarcation line in Europe; and the first thing, I think, that every reader will note is that their work does not divide on national lines and is entirely free of chauvinism or even national overtones. Neither I nor the other contributors would claim that it is a perfect work; but we hope that, as a pioneering effort, it will at least stimulate readers – particularly students and teachers – to reconsider some of their basic pre-suppositions about the nature, and what Oskar Halecki called the limits and divisions, of European history. We hope also that it will help them to realize that, in Frantisek Graus's words (p. 29), there are 'more important problems than frontier disputes, linguistic quarrels and national prestige', encourage them to concentrate on what the peoples of Europe have in common, and enable them to understand the forces which have bound them together, for all their national differences, in one community. If this book has any lesson to teach, it is that the time has come to widen our horizons. Concentration on the West, as though it were the sole repository of European civilization, may serve to harden our prejudices and fortify us in our belief in the superiority of our traditions; but it is a poor preparation for understanding the world in which we live.

'Those who call European civilization "western"', Oskar Halecki once wrote, 'are inclined to decide in advance one of the most difficult and controversial questions of European history.' Halecki was one of the first and leading proponents of the sort of revision at which this book aims, and if it were my book I should wish to dedicate it to him as a tribute to his long efforts to make the history of eastern Europe better known in the West. No doubt, the contributors to this volume would differ from him on a number of points of interpretation; but I hope nevertheless that it will serve the cause of better under-standing between the peoples of eastern and western Europe which – all politics apart – he has had so deeply at heart.

# I SLAVS AND GERMANS
*Frantisek Graus*


For the historian there are two traditional ways of dividing Europe: to classify its peoples from the linguistic, ethnic point of view as Germans, Latins and Slavs, or to regard cultural differences as the determining factors and to speak of West and East, of a Latin culture and a Greek culture, or of 'western values' in contrast to those of eastern Europe. In practice the two approaches frequently go hand in hand; and although most students of history appreciate that such classifications must not be taken too literally, the schematic approach shares the fate of other schemes that have become hallowed by tradition: it gradually becomes transformed into a prejudice. Past and present are interpreted in this spirit and as soon as the historian regards this approach as 'natural' he finds plenty of evidence to confirm it. Only when he begins to question his attitude to the past does he become aware of possible alternatives.

The need for a new approach has become increasingly apparent as a result of the great changes in the political balance between Europe and the extra-European world which have occurred since 1945. Suddenly the inhabitants of old Europe, intensely aware of the profound differences among themselves – differences they have come almost to regard as natural and God-given – appear in the eyes of the outside world as a unity, in contrast to Asia or Africa or America. We are confronted, in other words, with lines of division very different from those to which we are accustomed, and discover that the old national and racial groups – for example, Slavs and Germans – simply do not exist in the way we had thought. Nothing is easier than to endow the characteristics of a particular region with universal validity; but this can also be extremely deceptive. Very diverse peoples or tribes, for example, are collectively described as 'coloured' or 'white'. Such a grouping is obviously not entirely false, but it is crude and consequently misleading; what is wrong is that it tempts the historian to ignore basic differences within these groups, and that the labels soon acquire an emotional connotation and result in questionable judgments.

The historian who casts a critical eye at the historical map of Europe wonders immediately whether the racial and linguistic division of its peoples – sanctified by long and learned tradition – is correct or whether he is dealing with an indurated scholarly prejudice. As happens wherever human society is involved, the final verdict is unlikely to be clear-cut: he will, in other words, be able neither to confirm the old division nor simply to dismiss it as false. But by examining the origins of prejudices and the way in which they have gradually become revered tradition he can at least help to rectify mistakes and avoid bias. It is from this point of view that we shall, in the following pages, review the historical relations of the Slav and German peoples in the earlier centuries of European history.

DEVELOPMENT OF 'WESTERN' VIEWS
ABOUT GERMANS AND SLAVS

The Slavs are mentioned in ancient sources later than the Germans because these tribes came into contact with the Roman empire, then the centre of civilization, later than the Germans. In the first and second centuries AD there are references to the *Venedi*, the first Slavs mentioned in written records. Spreading through Europe they had by the middle of the first millennium settled more or less in the regions which they have inhabited since. Where these Slavs came from and who they were is a question to which the written sources give no answer.

The Slav settlement took place during the period usually described as the Barbarian Invasions, a time when new tribes of which the Romans knew little or nothing appeared suddenly in various parts of the Roman empire. In their descriptions the Romans followed the customs of earlier Greek ethnographers and gave the new peoples collective names as a means of

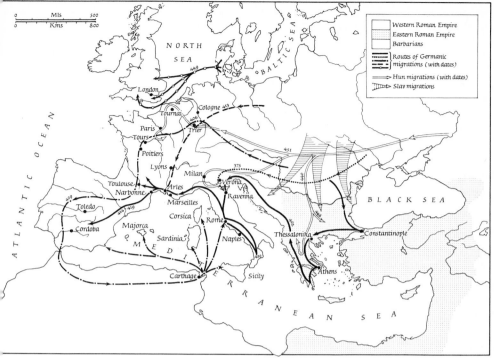

2 Tribal migrations in the fourth and fifth centuries.

classification. Thus it was the Romans who first referred collectively to the 'Germans', though to start with the name was given only to Germans 'civilized' by the Romans and not to 'free Germans' beyond the confines of the Roman world.

To the Romans all these new peoples were 'barbarians' and as such on a much lower level of civilization than the Greeks and the Romans. But even among Roman writers there were exceptions, among them Tacitus (d. AD 120) who idealized the unspoiled barbarian, and contrasted his alleged virtues with Roman decadence. Tacitus' model was the Germans. His idealized picture of them meets us in the pages of his famous *Germania*, and although the author himself later considerably qualified his idolization of the barbarians the book came to assume a role of fundamental importance in historical research; it became the hymn of praise of the ancient Germans, the basis of their subsequent glorification.

Among the Romans the Slavs found no panegyrist comparable to Tacitus, but later historical research was able to fall back on a Greek writer, Procopius of Caesarea (d. about AD 562), who spoke of 'democracy' among the Slavs. His viewpoint gained its supporters. About the origins of the Slavs, however, the ancient sources do not inform us. According to medieval legends they are supposed to have come to Europe from the south. But this view is undoubtedly based on the Biblical tradition that the different languages developed during the building of the Tower of Babel – consequently the Slavs, too, must have come to Europe from the Near East. About the way the Slavs really came to settle in Europe the legends tell us nothing, and the historical sources get us no further; like the origins of the Germans, the origins of the Slavs remain shrouded in mystery.

Nor has archaeological research penetrated the mystery. Although most archaeologists believe that there is a typically Slav type of pottery, it appears only in the fifth and sixth

3 Roman soldiers sack a village of the Marcomanni, a German tribe from Swabia; detail from the Column of Marcus Aurelius (AD 174).

4 Fourth-century Alemannic pottery and iron tools from a grave in Ilvesheim, near Mannheim.

5 Handmade Slav pottery of the fourth and fifth centuries, found in Poland.

centuries A D in central and parts of eastern Europe. Hitherto it has not been possible to relate these artifacts to older types as the exponents of the so-called 'autochthonic theory' have tried to do, nor to limit them to a particular geographical area. It is therefore not possible to prove that the Slavs gradually developed out of the pre-Slav local population (the autochthonic theory) nor to establish with certainty from where they came to the regions in which they later settled (the migration theory). If we compare 'the Slavs' and 'the Germans', the first thing to note is that there is a similar uncertainty about the origin of the Germans and about the archaeological demarcation line of their area of settlement, and this very fact casts doubt on the clear and precise division traditionally drawn between the two groups.

19

At this point we leave the classical sources and the archaeological evidence and turn to the histories of the Germans and the Slavs in search of clarification. These histories tell us less about what really happened than about how people imagined the past. But they do at any rate provide information about when and how people began to speak of 'the Germans' and 'the Slavs' as distinct groups and to make sweeping overall generalizations about them; and there is little doubt that these sweeping generalizations had a greater effect on the shaping of our ideas and prejudices than did the actual course of events.

The first to make such judgments were the ancient writers who collectively described a variety of different tribes whose languages struck them as being related as 'Germans', and who saw the movement of tribes as 'barbarian invasions'. This was the typical approach of the outside observer cataloguing part of the barbarian world from his own point of view and categorizing it in accordance with Roman ideas. These explanations, needless to say, had little, if any, significance for the German

6 German family travelling; 'metope' from the Trajanic monument of victory at Adamklissi in Rumania (first half of the second century).

tribes themselves, and though the Romans chose to regard them as a single people, they fought each other without scruple.

Medieval scholars inherited from Rome not only the descriptions of classical Latin writers but also the ideas of the ancient geographers and ethnographers. Confronted by a confusing variety of tribes and nations, the clergy, the intellectuals of the age, fell back on the models of ancient ethnographic literature and spoke of Germans and soon also of Slavs, because a linguistic affinity, particularly among the Slav tribes, was immediately apparent. A linguistically based national differentiation also developed in frontier regions where groups with different languages came face to face. But – and here we note the characteristic peculiarity of these names – the collective labels were almost without exception employed by outsiders. To be precise: German and French chroniclers and scholars spoke of 'Slavs'; Bohemian, Polish and Russian scholars spoke not of 'Slavs' (or, if they did so, they used the term to describe their own people alone) but of Bohemians, Poles or Russians (that is, of the particular tribe in question).

In addition, under Byzantine influence, there gradually began to grow up a literary concept of kinship among particular linguistic groups. This kinship, as was customary in the Middle Ages, was presented in the form of racial genealogies. In the thirteenth century we find the first attempt to exploit the idea politically. In 1278 when the Přemyslid king of Bohemia, Otakar II, was threatened by Rudolf of Habsburg, the German king, he addressed an appeal to the Poles which stressed the Slav kinship of the two peoples. But no sooner did the 'Slav' idea appear than its limitations became apparent. The Poles had naturally no idea of coming to the rescue of Otakar II; in the decisive battle against Rudolf on the Marchfeld in 1278 the Bohemian king was betrayed by the Czech nobles who had particularly strong 'national' feelings; and the author of the first political manifesto on Slav solidarity was an Italian notary who derived his ideas from classical sources. Towards the end of the Middle Ages there appeared various learned speculations

21

about the two great European racial families, the Germans and the Slavs; but these gained real importance only in modern times.

In this respect the rediscovery of Tacitus' *Germania* at the end of the fifteenth century was of particular significance, because Tacitus' idealized picture of the Germans fitted in with humanist scholars' ideas of an ideal society. But within the limits of the present essay we cannot stop to consider humanist and seventeenth-century scholarship in detail, although it was important as a first step. Modern research really starts in the eighteenth century with the beginnings of the new philology and the epoch-making work of Johann Gottfried Herder.

Herder (1744–1803) was the man who did most to shape later theories of the origins and divisions of the European peoples. Starting from an appreciation of everything 'natural', from the view that 'popular poetry' was more valuable than 'artificial poetry', he saw all nations as natural and equal partners in a great 'concert of peoples'. Whereas for the writers of the earlier Enlightenment, humanity in the abstract was the vehicle of historical progress, real peoples now assumed this role. In the famous sixteenth book of his *Ideen zur Philosophie der Geschichte der Menschheit* Herder prophesied a brilliant future for the Slavs because they were then particularly primitive (i.e. in Herder's view unspoilt) and because to him they seemed peace-loving by comparison with the Germans. Similar views had been voiced earlier, for example by the Bohemian J. A. Comenius (1592–1670), who attributed to his countrymen (in contrast to the Germans) the gentle ways of doves. But it was only in Herder's impressive formulation that these ideas were generally accepted.

Their victory was assisted by the growth of modern philology which distinguished between three great linguistic families in Europe: Latin, German and Slav. Language was the most 'natural', the 'basic' endowment of every people, transforming as it did a mere group, or agglomeration of individuals, into an organic people, or 'folk'. Not surprisingly, this idea was now transferred to the study of history. Because individual languages could easily be grouped into larger families it was thought that the same process could be applied to history. The theory broke down when it came to the so-called Latin peoples because the relatively late emergence of this entire group, the Roman contribution to its development and in particular the disappearance of the original languages of the later Latin peoples, were too obvious to make such assumptions possible. But as regards the Slavs and the Germans the equation seemed at first to work out perfectly.

In Germany a German interpretation was undertaken by the great scholars of the romantic age. The followers of the historical school of law invented a German law; Jacob and Wilhelm Grimm (1785–1863 and 1786–1859) discovered a German mythology and claimed to find fundamental German elements in the literature of particular peoples. Everything seemed to fit together in these fields, and it was generally thought that reconstruction would enable scholars to penetrate to the distant past, to the 'primordial' state. Parallel with attempts to discover through the historic languages an original Germanic or rather Indo-Germanic language, went efforts to find by the same method a German mythology, a German epic and a German law. Differences between particular historic German tribes were made light of so as not to disturb the alleged fundamental unity. Most attempts of this kind were based on late Scandinavian sources where historians thought that the old, 'original' German institutions had been preserved in uncorrupted form.

These notions were completely victorious in philology, and in the history of literature and law, and they dominated ideas generally, particularly in the form given them by Hegel in his *Philosophy of History* (not published until 1837). But attempts to reconstruct a common 'German history' on the model of language, mythology and law were doomed to failure. Efforts were made to demonstrate some sort of Germanic unity, at any rate for the late Roman period and the early Middle Ages; but even supporters of this theory of Germanic origins observed with regret that the 'ancient Germans' set little store by their alleged 'unity' and fought each other oblivious of ties of kinship or similarity of character. The complexity of relations between the different German tribes and foreign peoples, even in the early Middle Ages, was so obvious that attempts to construct a common 'German history' were left to amateurs. Serious historians paid due attention to the relations between Germanic and non-Germanic peoples, but still saw them, in accordance with current ideas, as contacts between distinct racial 'families'. The classical formulation of this view stemmed from Leopold von Ranke (1795–1886).

Ranke equated European history with western history and saw the history of Europe as a product of the Latin and the German peoples. It was this symbiosis which, according to Ranke, distinguished the occident (Europe) from other civilizations. Succeeding historians took over Ranke's interpretation; indeed, it was strengthened later in the nineteenth century as western readers became aware of the high artistic standard, the impressive quality, and the distinctive characteristics of the work of the Russian novelists. A different spirit, it was argued, infused Russian and 'western' literature; and the Russians were equated without qualification with the Slavs and sharply distinguished from the Germans and the Latins. Thus Europe was divided into two historical areas: a western area which was seen as populated by the Germans and the Latins, and an 'eastern' area which was identified with the Slavs.

Few historians were expert or knowledgeable enough to deal with Europe as a whole. The great majority confined themselves to the history of parts of the 'West' or of the 'East', the exact geographical limits of the 'West' being largely determined by the writers' origins and prejudices. There were also considerable differences in the assessment of the symbiosis which was supposed to have led to the creation of the 'West'. Some historians – again depending on their origins and political prejudices – gave greater emphasis to the Latin peoples, others to the Germans; some treated the Germans as a community of free men, others as an aristocratic society in which there were marked social differences from the very beginning. Scholars also differed in their views on the geographical boundaries of western culture and in the emphasis which they put on particular components. German nationalist historians tried to delimit exactly the German zone both in the West and in the East; for many Frenchmen the East began on the Rhine. But although Ranke's simple division was soon recognized to be out of date, the basic idea that people could be divided into linguistic groups survived. Historians continued to believe in the basic differences between 'West' and 'East' and in the possibility of dividing the European peoples into 'families'. It is only in recent times that this interpretation has broken down, although even now it has not really been abandoned, particularly in popular accounts and textbooks.

'EASTERN' VIEWS

We must now look briefly at the development of the concept of the Slav peoples among Slav historians, so as to see the way the ethnic idea operated on the other side. Here too the starting-point was the linguistic affinity which is much more apparent among the 'Slavs' than among the Germanic peoples and is immediately noticeable even to an untrained observer. Moreover, the 'Slav world' looked less fragmented than the rest of Europe and Herder's view of the greater spontaneity and freshness of the Slav peoples had obvious attractions for Slav writers. Therefore Herder was enthusiastically accepted in the Slav world; his chapter on the Slavs was translated more than once and even put into verse. But it soon became evident that any attempt to elaborate a common 'history of the Slavs' was confronted by insurmountable difficulties.

In philology, where Josef Dobrovský (1753–1829) had laid the foundations of solid research, the problem was relatively simple. And at first it seemed that the reconstruction of the general history of the Slavs in antiquity, for which Pavel Josef Šafařík (1795–1861) had done the spade-work, would be    25 equally straightforward. Suddenly historians discovered traces of Slavs everywhere in the ancient world, noted that they had once inhabited regions now occupied by other peoples, and regarded this fact as an historical injustice which filled them with melancholy and secret pride. But as they came to modern history and as they approached the present, their difficulties increased and the differences within the Slav world became more apparent than its common characteristics.

Looked at from outside, the superficial observer in the nineteenth century could still regard 'the Slavs' as a homogeneous whole; from within, however, the situation appeared very different. First of all there was the religious division: the east Slavs were Greek Orthodox, the west Slavs Roman Catholics, and in the case of the south Slavs the religious dividing line ran through the middle of their territory. Closely linked with the religious division was an analogous cultural division. But even more evident in the nineteenth century were the political and national differences. The only independent Slav country, Russia, was the most backward region in Europe, where serfdom continued until 1861 and where the non-aristocratic population had no privileges whatsoever. Very different was the social structure of Bohemia which had no indigenous aristocracy and whose civilization was markedly middle class. The biggest problem, however, was presented by the Poles whose country, after the third partition in 1795, had been divided among three neighbours. The heart of the old Polish state came under Russian rule, against which there were repeated Polish rebellions, heroic but unavailing. For the Russians (with the exception of a small group of 'Westernizers' who were little concerned with the historical scene) the Poles were therefore rebels and heretics, whereas for the Poles the Russians were heretics, tyrants and oppressors. These basic differences produced two fundamentally different views of the origins of Slav history, the only common factor being the idealization of the distant past.

For the Russian Slavophiles and the Russian exponents of the historic school of law, the tsar's rule was the natural climax of the whole of 'Slav' development, and the recipe which they offered to the other Slav peoples was simple: adopt the Greek Orthodox religion, take over the Russian alphabet and let yourselves be ruled by the tsar; in short, become as Russian as possible. This prospect understandably held little attraction for the more developed Bohemians and Poles. Moreover, it was important for the latter that their history should be presented in a way which did justice to the differences between them and the Germans. For the east Slavs this difference was less acute and less significant; Russia and Germany were usually friendly in the nineteenth century and in Russia people were far more concerned with the conflict with the Ottoman empire and Slav Poland than with the German question. It was therefore in the west Slav region that emphasis was laid on the age-old difference between Slavs and Germans.

The accepted interpretation of the difference between the Slavs and the Germans was advanced by two west Slav scholars: the Pole, Joachym Lelewel (1786–1861), and the Czech, Frantisek Palacký (1798–1876). Into the early period of Slav history – namely the tenth, eleventh and twelfth centuries – both projected an ideal of democratic rights, as such rights were seen by nineteenth-century liberals. The 'early Slav' period was presented as an idyll, destroyed by the so-called 'German colonization' in the thirteenth and fourteenth centuries. But at this point the differences between Bohemia and Poland became very apparent. In Poland, where the aristocracy (the *szlachta*) headed the national resistance movement against the foreign oppressor, Lelewel idealized the 'golden rights' of the Polish aristocracy and middle classes in early modern times by projecting them back into the distant past and thereby sanctifying them. In Bohemia, where the aristocracy played almost no role in Czech politics in the nineteenth century (it was overwhelmingly orientated towards Habsburg Austria), Frantisek Palacký proceeded more radically. In his view the old Slavs originally knew no class differences. From the start they formed a 'democratic society' of free men without aristocrats or serfs. 27

It was the 'German colonization' that brought this democracy to an end and it was under the influence of the Germans that aristocracy and serfdom were introduced. Fortunately, however, Bohemia and Poland found sufficient strength to resist complete Germanization, whereas hapless Slavs in the Elbe area became the booty of 'the Germans'.

Palacký's picture is more consistent and more memorable than Lelewel's, and for this reason it prevailed and became the generally accepted account. His theory was reinforced by forged sources of considerable artistic merit, the Königinhof and Grünberg manuscripts which were 'discovered' in Bohemia in 1817 and 1818 and which described a supposedly 'early' Slav world completely in line with Herder's idealization. In the second half of the nineteenth century, when these allegedly ancient sources were shown to be nineteenth-century forgeries, the accepted view had become too firmly entrenched to disappear completely. By and large it was retained, in modified form and without exaggerated idealization.

The concept of the 'democratic' Slavs had become an integral part of nineteenth-century scholarship; indeed it was accepted by German historians, even by nationalistic ones, although they interpreted it differently. What to Palacký and his followers was an idyllic form of democracy was seen by the Germans as a 'primitive state'. Accordingly the Germans were not brutal oppressors who had destroyed an idyll, but cultural pioneers who brought 'European civilization' to the primitive Slavs. Depending on the political and ideological standpoint of the historians concerned the Germans were presented as the bearers of western civilization or as the representatives of a 'Germanic spirit' that was incomparably superior to the Slav character. In either case the picture of 'the Slavs' and 'the Germans', and the contrast between them, had become stereotyped.

At the end of the nineteenth and the beginning of the twentieth century this view was shaken by a growing awareness of differences between the tribes and peoples collectively grouped together as 'the Germans' and those collectively grouped together as 'the Slavs'. Scandinavian scholars emphasized the purely hypothetical nature of the traditional picture of Germanic society, and archaeologists produced evidence that was irreconcilable with traditional views. Peoples between which hitherto little distinction had been made were now shown to have been endowed from the beginning with markedly individual traits. At the same time, the attempts to reconstruct a common 'German' or a common 'Slav' law as a basis for development floundered when it was found that many things that had formerly been regarded as specifically 'German' or specifically 'Slav' were common property. But the old traditions were too powerful and the political situation too tense to permit a complete reversal of the accepted view. Differences between Czechs and Germans in Bohemia and between Germans and Poles had become so acute after 1918 and the dividing lines between the particular camps so firm that any reference to possible flaws in the traditional arguments was regarded by both camps as a kind of 'national treason'.

After 1945 the situation greatly improved – let us hope permanently. Men saw with dismay where national passion had led them; they began to understand that Europe was no longer the centre of the world, and that there were more important problems than frontier disputes, linguistic quarrels and national prestige. This awareness is certainly not yet complete; national prejudices appear to be indestructible, like human stupidity. But if men can be brought to realize that the differences between them are relative, if they become more aware of the folly of national and racial prejudice, a step will at least have been taken in the right direction.

But it is not only awareness of the fundamental changes in the post-war world that has undermined the old approach to the question of 'the Germans' and 'the Slavs'. Historical research has also played its part. Historians who had long tried to make new facts fit in with old preconceptions began to realize that the presuppositions on which earlier research had been based were questionable. Opinions continue, of course, to differ on the extent to which traditional assumptions are in need of revision. But there is unanimity on the need to examine them anew in order to discover the sources of old mistakes. More precisely, we must look again at the old assumption that the European peoples can be divided into clear-cut racial groups and ask whether such a division is valid. We must see whether in historical times 'the Germans' and 'the Slavs' really constituted the sort of unity which the historian can use as a basis for interpretation.

'SLAV UNITY'?

The question of 'German unity' has long been a subject of controversy, particularly among German historians, many of whom have noted with disapproval the conflicts between different German tribes and regretted this 'fighting between brothers'. Though nobody today believes in 'German unity' of the sort postulated by late nineteenth-century historians, traces of this view still persist, tempting historians to assume some form of German unity in the distant past and to trace its continuity well into the Middle Ages. We cannot consider these views in detail here. Suffice it to say that, in my opinion, those historians are right who maintain that the whole concept of 'German unity' was thought up for specific purposes, originally by Roman writers with concrete political objectives in mind.

A few words are necessary, however, on the parallel concept of 'Slav unity' because there the sources are less well known and because to the present day the Slav peoples have remained linguistically more closely related than other comparable groups. If it can be proved in the case of 'the Slavs' that there is no justification for saying that different peoples must share in a common history because they speak similar languages, it will at least be a first blow to ethnic or racialist theories of historical development.

Even in the early Middle Ages chroniclers and writers used the collective description 'Slavs' (in a variety of spellings) in speaking of particular tribes. But they were usually aware of the often deep-seated differences between the various groups to which they gave this collective name. In the ninth century, for example, Einhard, the biographer of Charlemagne, listing the territories conquered by the emperor, refers to the west Slav tribes with whom Charlemagne had fought. He adds that these tribes 'while speaking almost the same language differ greatly (*valde dissimiles*) as regards customs and costume'. This fact was confirmed in the tenth century by the Arab-Jewish trader Ibrahim ibn Jaqub who travelled in Slav territory. He, too, observes that the Slavs consist of tribes which differ considerably from one another. But most contemporaries were not satisfied to describe tribes simply as 'Slav' but generally mentioned the specific tribal name. Even in the early Middle Ages, in short, men were struck by the similarity of language and the difference in customs.

Archaeology confirms this picture, although it is an open question whether the racial affinity of a particular tribe can be determined from archaeological material. This was long taken for granted, but scholars have now become more cautious although still using the assumption as a working hypothesis.

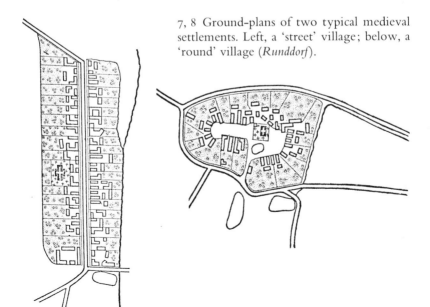

7, 8 Ground-plans of two typical medieval settlements. Left, a 'street' village; below, a 'round' village (*Runddorf*).

9 Model of the ninth-century Saxon 'Stellerburg' near Borgdorf.

10 Reconstruction of a twelfth-century castle of earth and timber at Lęczyca in Poland.

Already, however, it is clear that the search for a specifically Slav type of house, village or even of weapon is as unrealistic as the search for similar German prototypes. The construction of houses or the form of villages is determined primarily not by the origin or race of the settlers but by a number of specific factors: position, function, forms of husbandry, technical ability, and finally also by a tradition which is certainly neither 'Slav' nor 'German'. The 'German' and the 'Slav' house and village belong in the sphere of learned myths; in reality we find a great variety of forms in both cases.

Even more convincing are the results of the systematic post-1945 excavations in the west Slav region, which confirm the existence of a great variety of distinct stages of civilization. Whereas 'the Slavs' were once regarded as an amorphous mass without individual characteristics, archaeological investigations, particularly in the Kiev region, in western Poland and in southern Moravia, have revealed relatively advanced and

11 A hoard of coins, buttons and other objects buried after 925 and discovered in excavations at Obra Nowa, Poland.

12 Eastern influence
on Slav art: relief of
a lioness with her cub,
from Stara Zagora, Bulgaria
(seventh or eighth century).

13 Gold earrings from
Staré Město, an artistic
centre in the March valley
at the time of the Great
Moravian empire.

14 Early Slav jewellery,
including a fibula, earrings
and a bead necklace,
found in a sixth-century
grave at Szigetszenti-
miklós-Háros in Hungary.

34

distinct centres of civilization for which no common denominator can be found. Even the untrained observer cannot fail to note the difference between the south Slav finds and those made between the Elbe and the Saale, or the finds from the so-called Great Moravian empire (ninth century) and those from northern Slav territory.

There are also striking cultural differences. Ignoring religious divisions and the resulting differences, there is the known fact that the south Slavs and the east Slavs had an epic poetry, whereas there is no evidence of such literature in the west Slav region. As regards civilization as a whole, the region inhabited by the Slavs falls into different areas, and just as there is no one system of Slav law, so there is no uniform Slav civilization either. Even fairy-tales – a typical repository of folk culture – differ markedly from region to region.

What, finally, was the position in regard to political unity? Here, too, the historian finds frequent conflicts between Slav tribes, and like the German scholars who condemned the internecine struggles between German tribes, Russian, Czech and Polish historians were filled with despair by the Slavs' 'age-old hatred of their brothers'. But the facts are too palpable to be disposed of by later moral judgments.

Anyone approaching the question from a racial point of view would expect the strongest and oldest antagonisms to have existed at the 'Slav-German' frontier. But if we read the chroniclers of the two countries most exposed to German pressure, the Bohemians and the Poles, this is not the picture we get. The earliest Bohemian chronicler, Cosmas of Prague (d. 1125), regards the Poles as the Bohemians' worst enemies, and the so-called Gallus Anonymus (d. 1113), who wrote in Poland, sees the Bohemians as the Poles' worst enemy. And yet at that time there was still little difference between the language of the two peoples; they could at any rate understand each other without difficulty.

The picture is similar if we turn to the history of the west Slav tribes in the lands later conquered and annexed by the

Germans. Traditionally, subjection of these tribes – the Wends, the Sorbs, the Obodrites and others – was seen as a consequence of German-Slav antagonism and no attention was paid to the fact that they were attacked and enslaved from two sides: by the Germans and by the Poles. The conquered Slav inhabitants of these territories were repeatedly sold as slaves to Bohemia and Poland where no more reluctance to purchase and sell Slav prisoners of war was shown than, in an earlier age, was shown by Germans in buying and selling enslaved Scandinavians or at a later date by Italian merchants in trading in Christians from the Iberian peninsula.

One of the most important dividing lines in the 'Slav world' was religion, and Catholics and Greek Orthodox Christians accused each other of heresy, oblivious of any possible ties of kinship. Religious antagonism was naturally particularly strong between neighbouring peoples – for example, between Poles and Russians. But in the Middle Ages it was noticeable everywhere, because the church then made a far greater imprint on the cultural life of peoples than in more recent times. Nevertheless, the fact remains, that from whatever point of view we look at the concept of 'Slav unity' (and the same, it should be added, is true of 'German unity' in the Middle Ages) we find that the hypothesis fails to stand up to examination and has no real historical meaning.

It would, of course, be a mistake to deny any validity at all to the concepts 'Slavs' and 'Germans' and to claim that they are simply scholarly inventions. If nothing else, there is the fact of racial relationship which naturally made communication easier or more difficult. It is also a fact that at certain times and in certain areas people were conscious of Slav or German 'unity' and drew concrete political consequences from their awareness. All the present writer wishes to show is that German or Slav 'unity' is not axiomatic; the different nations do not fall 'naturally' into philologically definable groups according to their racial origins, and it is misleading to approach the problem from this angle.

The 'common feeling' of the Slavs (or the Germans) is not an 'inborn' feeling. In the earliest sources in particular this sentiment, if visible at all, is not in any way pronounced, and it was not until later, for the most part not until quite recent times, that it came to play a significant role. It is therefore necessary to distinguish clearly between linguistic similarities on the one side, and political and cultural differences on the other, and the postulate of unity, which has in modern times developed into a political ideology with all the consequences inherent in such a development. In other words, in examining the alleged unity of 'the Germans' and 'the Slavs' it is necessary to distinguish clearly between the actual course of history and its subsequent interpretation, between reality and wishful thinking, between learned theories and deliberate propaganda.

## SOCIAL STRUCTURE AND ORGANIZATION

If it is incorrect to assume that the Slavs and the Germans began their existence as distinct units and that there were from the beginning fundamental differences between these two 'families of peoples', it is because they have certain basic traits in common. A few examples will illustrate this fact. Nobody, for example, would claim today that Slav society at the beginning – unlike German – was 'democratic', i.e. that no social distinctions existed within it. The differences in grave furnishings discovered in excavations of Slav graveyards and the complicated fortifications of Slav castles amply confirm the existence of far-reaching social gradations in early Slav society, which are referred to in the written sources. The preconceived notion of the 'democratic' Slavs, the assumption that they were governed by assemblies of free men who met to determine the fate of their tribe by majority decision, misled earlier generations of scholars and tempted them to misinterpret the evidence.

From the time that the written sources allow us an insight into the internal structure of their society – that is, from the ninth century – there is ample evidence that the Slavs, like all other peoples, had ruling dynasties. Not every free warrior could be chosen as ruler by the community; only members of a certain clan, the royal dynasty, could rule. In the case of the south Slavs, we can deduce this fact only indirectly, but in the case of the so-called Great Moravian empire and of the empire of Kiev in the ninth century the sources provide clear proof, just as they do in the case of the Přemyslids in Bohemia and the Piasts in Poland. Moreover, accession to the throne was just as much a decisive symbolic act in the so-called Slav world as it was in the West. Both the existence of a noble class and the fact that members of the royal dynasty alone could rule are common to both the 'Slavs' and the 'German' peoples, and show how hard it is to draw a dividing line between the two.

Nor is this the only similarity in social and political institutions. Recent research, correctly in the author's view, sees in the rulers' retinue the most important germ cell of the early medieval state. It was the prince's retinue that constituted his strength and formed the basis of his rule, not the mythical tribal contingent of free men on which nineteenth-century historians placed such stress. The allegiance owed by the retainers to the ruler differed considerably according to circumstances, as did the forms of recompense of the vassals – but here again racial factors were not of fundamental significance. What was decisive was the way the retinue was organized and the way in which the vassals became members of the medieval aristocracy. There were no characteristically 'German' or 'Slav' types of retinue and it is equally mistaken to assume that the 'German retinue' was bound together by some sort of blood tie (the so-called 'German loyalty'). We can see how varied the forms were if we compare the retinue of the Vikings and the Franks, both allegedly 'Germanic', and the retinue of the Bohemian and the Kiev rulers, both allegedly 'Slav'. The difference between the two former and between the two latter are just as great as any differences between the 'Slav' and the 'German' groups. In short, the differences in the structure of royal retinues depended not on language or racial affinities but on a variety of concrete factors which do not have to be considered here.

The same is true of the early medieval state. Just as there is no characteristically 'German' or 'Latin' state, so there is no characteristically 'Slav' state either. To illustrate this point it is only necessary to compare the development of England, the Empire and Denmark in the early Middle Ages, countries which from a linguistic point of view all belonged to the Germanic world, but whose development was so different that it is impossible without a complete distortion of the facts to speak of a 'Germanic state'. Similarly, in the ninth and tenth centuries Arab-dominated Spain on the one hand and France and Italy on the other – the nomenclature is anachronistic but is used for the sake of simplicity – have so little in common that it is senseless to describe them collectively as 'Latin states'. The same is true, although the fact is not generally appreciated except by specialists, of the 'Slav states'; the Kiev principality, Croatia and Bohemia have little more in common in the ninth century than the western European states mentioned above.

15, 16 Left, bronze helmet of a Frankish prince (c. 600), found with his weapons and treasure in a grave at Morken, Germany. Right, Frankish jewellery from the sixth-century grave of a noblewoman in Güdingen, Germany.

Comparative history can certainly discover analogies and parallels but it is these very parallels that explode the theory of the ethnic division of the peoples of Europe. In the early Middle Ages a distinct group, closely related in structure, is formed by the states of Bohemia, Poland and Hungary; but these states are no more ethnically homogeneous than were the closely linked western and eastern parts of the Frankish empire in the ninth century.

Space does not permit us to enlarge on these facts; but if they are accepted, the division of peoples into those that were capable of forming states and those that were not becomes totally nonsensical, and the theory (once popular in Germany) that the Slavs were somehow constitutionally incapable of setting up states of their own is as unacceptable as the view that all Slav dynasties must have been of native 'Slav' origin. The futility of such arguments is illustrated by the fact that states were formed in the Slav world at a time when there was no similar political organization in 'Germanic' Scandinavia; and there is as much evidence of the rule of foreign conquerors in the Slav part of the world as, for example, in Celtic Britain or in Gallo-Roman France, or other countries of the West. Such arguments simply apply romantic and sentimental prejudices to the early Middle Ages and distort historical reality by projecting modern chauvinism back into the distant past.

The story of the conversion of the different European tribes to Christianity also confirms the view that any attempt to group them on linguistic lines in the early Middle Ages is illusory, as a few examples will show. The closest parallel to the conversion of the Russians on the insistence or orders of their ruler is found in Scandinavia. The conversion of Bavaria proceeded entirely differently from that of Iceland, and there are no similarities worth mentioning between the course of events in the principality of Kiev and that in Bohemia. Particularly significant is the case of Moravia, the scene of activity of the two brother missionaries, Cyril and Methodius, who introduced the

Slavonic liturgy there. After Methodius' death in AD 885 his disciples were expelled by the Moravian ruler, Svatopluk, who was in a constant state of war with Arnulf, ruler of the east Frankish empire.

It is modern historians who, over-emphasizing the national aspect, have 'discovered' an apparently racial and national impulse behind the story of the conversion. In reality, there was no more a 'conversion of the Slavs' than there was a 'conversion of the Germans'. Just as Christianity came to the Franks in one way and to the Saxons in another, so the conversion of the Bohemians and of the Slav peoples beyond the northern borders of Bohemia took completely different courses. The Slav region was divided in religion almost from the start. Whereas it was not until the Reformation in the sixteenth century that the German lands were split into two religious areas, the burning of the pope's bull of excommunication by the assembled prelates in the cathedral of St Sophia at Constantinople in 1054 meant not only the final break between Constantinople and Rome but also sealed the religious and cultural split of the so-called 'Slav world'.

17 Frankish warrior on a late seventh-century funeral stele combing his hair, symbolizing the survival of the forces of life; the double-headed serpents surrounding his head represent the forces of darkness who take the dead into their realm.

41

More examples could easily be cited. One might point, for instance, to the different levels of cultural development of particular regions and show how impossible it is to attribute these differences to racial factors. One might examine the great movement of European colonization and land reclamation which lasted for centuries and linked up the settlement areas of separate tribes, thus creating the landscape with which we are familiar. One might point out that part of this story of colonization – the so-called German *Drang nach Osten* – has been taken out of its context and interpreted (or rather misinterpreted) from a nationalist point of view. But this cannot be done in a short essay; a whole book would be needed for the purpose.

Sufficient has been said, however, to show that it is grossly misleading to transfer the categories of linguistics or purely geographical division, to the history of peoples. The abstractions of 'Slav' and 'German' or 'western' and 'eastern' history simply do not correspond to the facts; if anything they have helped to erect barriers and strengthen prejudices. The early history of Europe is not overshadowed by antagonism between Germans and Slavs, nor can it be reduced, in the spirit of Ranke, simply to a symbiosis of the German and the Latin peoples. The tribes and peoples from which the early medieval states of Europe developed as germ cells of the future nations, had much in common from the outset – as well as being very different. The nations developed by influencing as well as by fighting each other. None can be considered in isolation, nor can they be reduced to language groups or racial 'families'. Only when we throw away the blinkers of the traditional approach to the early history of Europe shall we see it for what it really was: a melting-pot from which the states and nations of Europe emerged, assimilated by long contact and interaction, but still at odds with one another.

# II POLITICAL RELATIONS BETWEEN EAST AND WEST

*Karl Bosl*

Throughout the Middle Ages, for obvious geographical reasons, the peoples of eastern Europe who were in closest contact with the West were the west, and to a lesser degree the south Slavs. This does not mean that the Baltic provinces or the Russian empire of Kiev can be left out of account. The influence of Byzantium, which prevailed in the Kiev region, was always important. And it was not only with their immediate neighbours, the Germans, that the Slavs were in contact. All the western peoples, including the Anglo-Saxons, had relations at one time or another with eastern Europe; these extended from commerce to dynastic marriages. But it hardly needs demonstrating that the most intensive relations were those between the west Slavs and their westerly neighbours: the Germans. German-Slav relations left the most lasting mark, and here we can distinguish four periods, or phases.

The first begins with the westward movement of the Slav tribes in the sixth century, against which Charlemagne organized a system of marches on the eastern frontiers of his empire. The second stage is marked by the rise of autonomous Slav states on the eastern flank of the Holy Roman Empire – sometimes in loose connection with, or tributary dependence upon it – during the ninth and tenth centuries; this period is the one which east European historians often looked back to as the 'golden age' of the Slav nations before their renaissance after 1918. The third period of relations is characterized by the German eastward movement, the *Drang nach Osten*, beginning in the second half of the eleventh century. This German eastward movement was fundamentally different from the earlier westward movement of the Slavs, in so far as the territories the Slavs occupied were for all practical purposes vacant, whereas the Germans came face to face with a settled and civilized population, with which they had been in contact, sometimes friendly, sometimes hostile, for at least two or three centuries. Finally, the German eastward thrust resulted in a Slav reaction, which ushered in the fourth period. In the last century of the Middle Ages, revolts and revolutions under national kings and princes brought to an end an interval of government under foreign rulers – the Luxembourg dynasty in Bohemia, for example, or the Angevin dynasty in Hungary – whose rule had been characterized by intensive contacts, not only with Germany but also with the nations – France and Italy – west and south of the German Reich.

It was, no doubt, a consequence of the lines of historical development outlined above that the Germans stood out, in the eyes of the Slavs, as the enemies and aggressors. This attitude, anchored in the ideology of the so-called 'Slavic legend', was reinforced after the end of the Middle Ages by the fact that it was the Prussians and Austrians – joined, after the time of Peter the Great, by Russia – who became the dominant powers throughout the east European borderlands.

THE WESTWARD MOVEMENT OF THE SLAVS

From the sixth century onwards Slav tribes immigrated into the vast territories east of the Elbe and the Saale, the Bohemian Forest and the river Enns in Austria, which the Germanic tribes had left after having settled there for many centuries. These early German tribes were different from the inhabitants of medieval Germany, just as the Anglo-Saxons were different from them, or from the Romanized Franks in Gaul. The German eastward movement of the twelfth and thirteenth centuries is therefore in no sense a resettlement of ancient German territory, for Germany as a nation did not exist before the end of the ninth century.

The original homelands of the Slavs were on the rivers Dnieper, Pripet, Bug and Vistula. They started from there in big movements westward; about AD 500 they reached the

18 The Slav states in the ninth century and the kingdoms of Poland, Bohemia and Hungary (*c.* 1400).

territories on the lower Danube and moved forward along the river and to the south and west into the valleys of the eastern Alps. But they lost their independence very soon, for the Avars, nomadic breeders of cattle, subjected the agrarian Slavs who moved under their pressure and influence not only into Bohemia and Moravia, but also into the lands of the Sorbs north of the Sudeten mountains and into the territory around the river Main west of the Bohemian Forest.

45

As these movements and settlements proceeded, corresponding types of lordship and state came into existence. In the south the states were not tribal – that is to say, built up on the foundation of family groups and family settlements – but were rather lordships, in which one leader united different tribal remnants with the aid of a group of warriors, who secured him control of market-places and highways of traffic. In the north-west, on the contrary, dominion was based on well-defined tribal groups, such as the Vilzi, Obodrites or Sorbs. We may compare these incipient states with the tribal formations of Germanic Europe, the former with the so-called war-kingdoms of the migration period, the latter with the Germanic tribal groups on the Rhine, the Weser and the Elbe, as described by Tacitus. But the Slavs who had crossed the Elbe and the Saale and the Bohemian Forest, and had settled there on the soil of the Frankish empire, failed to build up lasting political organizations and were unable to preserve their independence. They were not enslaved, but lived in a status similar to the 'Königsfreien' and other tenants (*coloni*) of the Frankish empire, not only in Thuringia and Old Saxony, but also in the upper Main valley.

It seems probable that the early lordships in the Slav lands arose under Frankish influence. Samo, founder of an empire between the Sudeten mountains and the eastern Alps, was of Frankish descent; we may surmise that he was a slave trader, for Slavs were enslaved throughout the early Middle Ages and sold at slave markets such as Venice, Verdun or Regensburg. Derwan, the duke of the Sorbs, a contemporary of Samo, had also acknowledged Frankish supremacy. Frankish influence is traceable in the ninth century among the Vilzi and the Obodrites, and Franks helped Pribina to build up his power in the region of the Plattensee in modern Hungary. But we must realize that such influences were neither strong nor continuous; only a few specifically Frankish institutions were transferred, which did not substantially alter the original Slav foundations. We should not forget, either, that our information comes from Frankish sources which present us with only one side of the picture.

The first Slavs to found an empire were the tribes of Moravia, united under the rule of the descendants of Moimir. The centre of their kingdom was the valley of the river March, where excavations carried out since 1945 by the archaeologists of the Czechoslovak Academies of Prague and Bratislava have yielded impressive evidence, in the form of fortifications, towns, churches and so on, of a relatively high and developed civilization. We can trace the beginnings of this so-called Great Moravian empire before Charlemagne, who decisively defeated the Avars by a concentric attack on their central position on the river Theiss. The ancient Roman province of Pannonia, comprising western Hungary and modern Yugoslavia, was a vast field for the interplay of cultural and ecclesiastical movements from east, south and west, and here the Moravian rulers tried to build up an independent position between the powers of their age, the Byzantine empire, the Carolingian empire in the west,

19 Foundations of a ninth-century palace in Mikulčice, probably the political centre of the Great Moravian empire.

20, 21 Above, ground-plan of an early ninth-century rotunda from Mikulčice; the horseshoe shape of the two apses suggests eastern stylistic influence. Left, sixth-century silver plate, probably south Russian, with an ornamental design based on the typical eastern palmette motif.

and the Roman church. The arrival of the Magyars in the ninth century destroyed the domination of the descendants of Moimir in the eastern part of modern Czechoslovakia. But it seems that, as late as the end of the ninth century, Prague and its rulers still obeyed the last Moravian ruler, Svatopluk, and so the influence of Moravian civilization persisted in this region and was still an effective force in medieval Bohemia, for instance in the monastery of Sázava.

In the eastern Alps the Slavs succeeded in erecting an autonomous 'state', which was called later Carantania, or Carinthia. We do not yet know exactly what role the Croats played in this development. Carinthia was later incorporated into the duchy of Bavaria and so into the Carolingian empire. The Croats were the first Slavs to build up a strong autonomous 'state' in the southern parts of central Europe, in Pannonia and Dalmatia. Their rulers Ljudevit and Borna were dangerous opponents of the western empire and the Croats preserved their independence until 1091.

22 Magyars attacking a fortified town; drawing from the *Book of Maccabees*, produced *c.* 924 in St Gallen.

The political independence of eastern Europe, and the formation of a distinctive society there within the framework of medieval Christian civilization was largely the result of the development of three states in the ninth, tenth and eleventh centuries: Bohemia and Poland, both Slav, and Hungary, the main element in the population of which was not Slav, but Finno-Ugrian and Turco-Tatar. The Czechs, first named in 806 in a Frankish source, gained control over Bohemia under the rule of the Přemyslids, who subjected or eradicated the minor lords and castellans throughout the country. This process was completed by 995, when the Slavnikids, their chief rivals, were eliminated by murder. The castle of Prague was the centre of Přemyslid dominion and became the capital of the country for a thousand years.

This Czech or Bohemian 'state' was characterized by strong internal cohesion, a sign of effective rulership. Although Franks and Germans influenced its development and although its territory was included in the Bavarian bishopric of Regensburg as a missionary district, none of this was decisive and it did not interfere with the individual shaping of this extraordinary kingdom. Modern Czech nationalist historians have rejected the fact that Bohemia was more or less closely linked with the German empire since the tenth century; but such a linkage did occur and was the consequence of the organization of a Bohemian territorial church about 973, when the bishopric of Prague was founded and united with the German imperial church as part of the metropolis of the archbishopric of Mainz. It was Charles IV, German emperor and king of Bohemia in the middle of the fourteenth century, who secured the elevation of Prague into an independent archbishopric and gave his country a short, but virtually complete independence for a period of one and a half centuries. Slav Bohemia became one of the most highly developed 'territorial states' in advance of all other German territories, and it is equally significant that, as in Hungary and Poland, the crown came to symbolize an objective and impersonal idea of the state earlier than in Germany. This fact indicates the inherent statesmanlike qualities of the west Slavs. In spite of being a nominal member of the Empire, Bohemia never became merely one among the many territorial states of which the Empire was composed.

Poland and Hungary, the two other leading states of east central Europe, stood for only a very short time·under the suzerainty of the German emperors of the Saxon line. Both quickly succeeded in gaining complete independence. The Magyars, nomadic horsemen who terrorized Europe for half a century and devastated parts of Saxony, France, Italy and the Byzantine empire, were compelled by their defeat in 955 at the battle of the Lech to change their way of living and to settle down in the plains along the Danube and the Theiss where they ruled over an indigenous population of Slavs. The fact that they did not accept the Christian faith from Byzantium, but adopted the western and Roman liturgy and ritual, was of decisive importance, although they postponed their final decision for some decades. The Magyars celebrate Stephen I as the founder and hero of the Hungarian state; although the details are not very clear, it is beyond dispute that he was proclaimed king by both emperor and pope.

In the second half of the tenth century Mieszko I united a number of Slav tribes east of the Oder under his rule and in this way founded the original Polish state. The centre of his realm was round Kruszwica, Gniezno and Poznań; from here he began to expand his political dominion over Bohemia, Cracovia and Silesia, and after 990 over Pomerania also. By formally placing his territories under the suzerainty of St Peter he won the acknowledgment of his position by the Holy See. Significantly the account of this transfer, called 'Dagome iudex' from its opening words, sets out exactly the frontiers of the territories under Mieszko's rule, thus indicating that in Poland also the concept of a territorial state with fixed borders existed from the beginning. Mieszko acknowledged the supremacy of the German kings, but he pursued a completely independent policy, not least of all in his relations with the Roman church,

and this policy was continued by his son Boleslav I Chrobry, 'the Mighty' (992–1025). Whether the ruling family of Piasts was of Viking descent or not, cannot be confirmed or disproved. But the newly founded Polish archbishopric of Gniezno (A D 1000) became an independent metropolitan province of the universal church and this act simultaneously opened the way for political independence.

The German emperor Otto III (983–1002) and his clerical advisers saw the need to establish some sort of order among the newly rising states in eastern Europe. One of the objects of Otto III's policy of 'Renovatio', or the renewal of the ancient Roman empire, it has been suggested, was to make a place for western Slavs as members of the Empire with equal rights under the suzerainty of the German king. This particularly affected the Poles who apparently were thought to hold the dominant position in this area. But with the early death of Otto III the rather vague idea of a universal Christian empire over the whole of central and eastern Europe collapsed. Boleslav Chrobry pursued an independent policy of his own. In his eyes the foundation of the archbishopric of Gniezno and his designation

23 Above left, King Stephen I (977–
1038) of Hungary in coronation
robes; detail of a manuscript page
from the Hungarian *Picture
Chronicle* (second half of the
fourteenth century).

24 Above, coffin of Stephen I,
who died in 1038.

25, 26, 27 Above left, coin of
Boleslav I Chrobry (992–1025),
minted before 1000, bearing the
inscription PRINCEPS POLO-
NIE (obverse side). Compare a
similar coin (centre left) minted
in 1000, bearing the inscription
GNESDUM CIVITAS (obverse
side), and commemorating the
granting of the title of king to
Boleslav by Otto III at Gniezno.
Below left, dinar of Mieszko I of
Poland.

53

as the emperor's 'cooperator mundi' and 'associate and friend' did not mean the inclusion of Poland in a universal Christian empire ruled by the Roman-German emperor, but liberation of the Polish church from the control of a German metropolitan and full freedom of action for the growing Polish state. When in 1002, after the death of Otto III, Boleslav launched an attack on the Empire and temporarily occupied the march of Meissen, the ruler of the young Polish state made clear that he was not willing to accept a situation which prevented him from attacking his neighbours, particularly Bohemia, and attempting to unite the Slav peoples of the area in a strong state under Polish leadership. The policy of Otto III had failed.

Nevertheless, although asserting their political independence, the new powers in the east of central Europe – Poland, Hungary, Bohemia – were all influenced in one degree or another by contact with the Empire. They had peaceful as well as hostile relations with their neighbours in the West. Although the rising states of eastern Europe were overshadowed by the Empire, Slavs and Germans not only fought, but also compromised and co-ordinated their interests. In particular, the Christianization and ecclesiastical organization of the three eastern European states prevented the West from waging missionary war against them; as a result of their conversion they obtained equal religious rights and equal status as autonomous members of Christendom. Although the missionaries came from outside, especially from German bishoprics, Christianization was not carried out by the sword but took place in agreement with the native princes and magnates. This voluntary religious decision prepared the way for a voluntary integration into the political system of medieval Europe.

The invasion of the Magyars and their settlement in the plains of Hungary had separated the world of the Slavs into a western and a southern group. The south Slavs in the Balkans and in the Danube area and the eastern Alps reacted in the same way as their western brothers against pressure from the West; that is to say, they voluntarily accepted the Christian faith. The

28 Otto I (912–73) presents a model of Magdeburg cathedral to Christ in majesty on a tenth-century ivory plaque.

29 Otto III (980–1002) in imperial robes, seated on his throne; from an ivory holy-water stoup (*c.* 1000).

Slav tribes between the Elbe, the Saale and the Oder, on the other hand, had a different fate. Many of them were later forcibly converted to Christianity from Germany, others – especially in the regions south of the Baltic Sea – from Poland. They were subjected to German domination, though only after bitter struggles with Poland for control of the area. The archbishopric of Magdeburg had been established as a missionary centre for the Slavs beyond the Elbe in the time of the emperor Otto I. In this early period no clear distinction was drawn between religion, politics and missionary activities; and it is undeniable that missions were frequently used as an instrument of policy, not only by the Germans but also by the Poles under Boleslav I. But the classic instances of the use of religion to enforce political control came later with the so-called 'crusade' or German missionary war against the Wends in 1147 and the subjection of the heathen Prussian tribes on the Baltic by the Teutonic knights in the thirteenth century.

The Slav tribes in this area also had to face growing pressure from the marches which Charlemagne had organized along the eastern borders of his empire, and which were later extended. The German ruler Henry I (919–36) conquered Brandenburg and established the march of Meissen. His son Otto I organized new marches east of the Elbe and the Saale. The Magyar onslaught had shattered the defences along the Carolingian frontier in the south-east; so the same ruler took measures here also to restore the frontier system under new margraves or 'marchiones'. In this area the German bishoprics continued to control the territory beyond the frontier; but in the north-east new bishoprics were erected in the newly created marches.

Otto I's aggressive policy in the eastern marches of Saxony and the forced Christianization which accompanied it, provoked the great rebellion of the Slavs in 983, which had even more serious repercussions than the invasion of the Magyars in the south. German domination between the Elbe and the Oder north of Magdeburg broke down completely and could not be restored in spite of many military campaigns. A number of small Slav principalities were set up in the liberated areas and managed to survive for a short period without being Christianized. The majority of the tribes stubbornly resisted missionary activity. Since bishoprics had once been established here and then destroyed, these people were not pagans in the eyes of rulers and clergy; they were therefore declared renegades, who were to be guided back to the true faith by force. But in the area south of Magdeburg, in the so-called Middle Germany of today, the Germans succeeded in maintaining their hold over the inhabitants, mostly Slavs, but scarcely Christians. The Slavs in the south-eastern territories of the Empire, in the eastern Alps and along the Danube also lost their independence. Ever since Carolingian times, but particularly after Otto I's defeat of the Magyars in 955, there was a continuous admixture of German settlers and the native population was intensively Christianized. In Bohemia, on the other hand, there were only a few German settlers; the Czech character of the people was untouched and native dukes ruled the country virtually independently, although formally Bohemia was a member of the western empire.

Acceptance of the Christian faith made the Slavs a part of the growing Christian society of Europe. By adopting the progressive institutions of the greater powers and by imitating their standards of civilization and accepting the Christian faith, the Slav princes built up their reputation at home, reinforced their power abroad, and secured their political independence. The strength and genius of individual rulers and their decision to follow the model of western institutions in state and church definitely united the Slav tribes in effective states. This was the case not only with the Czechs, Poles and Magyars, but also with the eastern Slavs in the empire of Kiev during the tenth century. Here also western influences were stronger than is often allowed, and it was not yet certain in the tenth century whether Kiev would follow the Byzantine or the Roman ritual and liturgy. It was no accident that in the Gospel of Otto III, in the famous miniature in which figures representing the four parts of the Empire do homage to the emperor, 'Sclavinia' took its place beside 'Roma', 'Gallia' and 'Germania' as the fourth member of the western Christian community. By the end of the first millennium the Slavonic East was an integral part of the European world.

Another consequence of these events was that none of these nations ever again lost its individuality and its distinctive character. The Croats lost their national dynasty shortly before 1100 and from that time forward were ruled by the Hungarian dynasty and associated with Hungary in a personal union. On the other hand, the Serbs, living in the central mountains of the Balkans, succeeded in spite of many political fluctuations in building up a wall consisting of their own and other peoples around their often endangered state. Under the leadership of Stefan Dušan (1331–55), Serbia entered on a period of great achievement and importance, shortly before the Turks invaded the Balkan peninsula. And native dynasties ruled Bohemia,

Poland, Hungary and Russia until the fourteenth century or later. These dynasties, the Přemyslids and Piasts, the Arpads and the Rurikids, had major achievements to their credit. It was due to them that, from the beginning of the second millennium, their kingdoms were able to stand on their own feet and keep back the political pressures and cultural penetration of foreign powers. They rejected the universal pretensions of the German emperors, took over the tasks of civilizing their subjects and set about improving the living standards of their own people.

The western emperor had lost his commanding position in eastern Europe by the close of the eleventh century; the Byzantine empire was also losing its influence in the Slav world. From the time of Boleslav Chrobry the pagan Baltic tribes came under missionary influence from Poland. Much the same happened in the area inhabited by the south Slavs, which the Hungarian rulers tried to annex to their dominions, organizing a system of marches along the frontiers and south of the Danube against invasions from outside. In the pagan Baltic area Polish and Russian rulers co-operated from the eleventh century onwards.

Ecclesiastical and political developments in the new states of eastern Europe bear witness to steady cultural interchange between East and West, especially between the western Slavs and Hungary on the one side, and Germany on the other. But there were also direct communications with France and Italy, which indicate the independent position and reputation of these nations within the Christian society of Europe.

There is no better example of the progress of culture in the eastern world than Kiev. Russian literature developed under Byzantine and Bulgarian influence during the eleventh century, and many important literary documents – among them we find testimonies of the missionary activities of Cyril and Methodius and their pupils in Moravia – came to Kiev from the West. Kiev was linked with the West by relatively intensive trade and commercial relations. Regensburg in Bavaria and its citizens continued to trade with Kiev and its empire for more

30 Main apse of the Hagia Sophia, Kiev (1037), with the Virgin Mary praying in the semi-dome and, below, Christ administering Holy Communion to the Apostles.

than two hundred years. There were also intensive commercial relations between Kiev, Prague and Poland. The Rurikids showed special interest in the fields of architecture, literature, historiography and legislation. The 'Paučenije' of Prince Vladimir Monomach (1113–25) is an impressive testimony of human and political wisdom.

## THE GERMAN EASTWARD MOVEMENT

The end of the early Middle Ages and the supersession of the primitive society of early medieval Europe was marked in the eleventh century by a rapid growth of social mobility. This new mobility ushered in a period of expansion beyond the old frontiers of Europe, both in the Mediterranean and east of the Empire, as well as a vast process of internal colonization, the clearance of forests and the draining of swamps, in the old areas of settlement. The crusades in the south and the eastward thrust of the Germans in the north were the two outstanding events in this process of change which was taking place in the whole of Europe. The archaic feudal society was not dissolved, but its character was changed and broadened in essential ways by the rise of a new middle class, the citizens, and the structure of European society was enriched by a new kind of urban civilization.

Human, social, commercial, and political life was concentrated in the new towns and cities, developed from pre-urban settlements, which we find among the Slavs as well as in the Latin and German parts of Europe. The new social and economic movements, themselves a consequence of a population surplus, the new settlements and a progressive urban civilization initiated a third period of political relations between East and West. The centres of this movement were Italy, Flanders and south and west Germany. There is no doubt that the East gained new impulses and strength from the new movements, the power of the east European states was intensified, East and West drew closer together, and an intensive assimilation of standards took place. The Danes and Swedes, heirs of Viking tradition, also participated in this movement, but the Germans played the most important part.

This process of assimilation was a decisive development in European history; but for the Slavs, at least up to recent times, its negative aspects have loomed larger than the positive ones. The reason, of course, is that during this period not only were vast Slav territories in the western border zone lost to the Germans, but also a new political order was established between the Baltic Sea and the Danube valley which fundamentally altered the situation of the east European states. In the West, on the other hand, especially among the Germans and German historians, the conviction gained ground that it was only at this time and as a result of 'Germanization' that the Slavs acquired the foundations of higher civilization, by the assimilation of the more progressive techniques of the West, by the acceptance of western standards in social, economic, legal and spiritual life, and especially by the penetration into the Slav lands of the urban civilization of Germany.

If such views could prevail, it was in part at least because vast territories in the east of the Slav world were lost to sight by the West as a result of the establishment of Tatar or Mongol domination in the thirteenth century and the rise of the centralized state of Moscow. In reality, the German eastward movement in the thirteenth and fourteenth centuries was successful only because the Slavs were already Christians and already had civilized standards; reluctant, hostile and pagan barbarians would not have been able or willing to accept the new progressive way of life. The rulers of eastern Europe were interested in reforming the economy and the social structure of their countries, in order to be able to compete with the West, and for this purpose they invited western settlers, artisans, miners and traders to settle in their kingdoms.

Poland is the best example of these trends. The growing population surplus in Poland made it possible, even necessary, to cultivate new land, especially to open up the forests within the Polish frontiers. With this land policy the princes combined large-scale efforts to increase the military and financial power of their country by internal colonization and urbanization. But the effects of internal colonization were limited if carried out according to existing Polish law. What was necessary, if the legal and economic situation were to be improved, was a shift in balance between rights and duties, between the rights of the urban and rural classes involved in the colonizing movement and those of the government; and this could not be secured by any measures available in Slav legal tradition. Hence the Polish rulers turned to German methods of colonization, inviting western settlers into the country and granting them privileges. Colonization was carried out according to German law; and the success of this method in solving the difficulties and meeting the requirements of the situation is indicated by the fact that the privileges of German law were also granted to Slav peasants and settlers.

In this way the economic, social and legal order of eastern Europe was improved and reformed. Later, in the fifteenth century, the same methods were applied in the Russian-settled territories of the Polish-Lithuanian Union. Colonization and the opening up of new land were successful, because the application of German law and methods enabled the Slav nations to introduce a new measure of social differentiation and a broader cultural base. Looked at from this point of view, we can see that the effects of the so-called German eastward move-ment were not confined only to the extension of German national territory, but had important consequences for the internal development of the Slav states, and played their part in the shaping of European civilization. They helped to secure economic stability and a balanced social order not only in Poland, but also in Bohemia and Hungary. On this foundation rulers such as Přemysl Otakar II and Charles IV of Bohemia, Casimir the Great of Poland and the Angevin kings of Hungary won a high reputation for statesmanship throughout Europe.

The resistance of the western Slavs and Hungarians, who
could not be defeated by force and war, prevented the German

31 The castle of Marienburg was the seat of the grand master of the Teutonic Order from 1309.

kings from conquering their territories by direct assault. In part this failure was a result of the swampy terrain of north-east Europe. But it was also a proof of the material and moral strength and of the spirit of freedom of the small and often mutually hostile Slav tribes between the Elbe and the Oder. But the medieval German settler movement beginning at the end of the eleventh century, an event comparable with the American westward movement and settlement of the nineteenth century, eventually Germanized this area. The immediate result was expansion of German domination and the dissemination of western political, legal and economic institutions in a German form, as well as of western science, poetry and art. But it was the assimilation of these institutions by the countries

63

involved that has shaped the cultural face of central and eastern Europe from that time down to the present day.

The settlement of German townsfolk and peasants was not met by force by the Slavs as the earlier military attacks had been. Kings, dukes and princes in Hungary, Bohemia, Silesia, Mecklenburg, Pomerania and Poland all supported the colonizing movement, and the German immigrants were given effective aid by the crown, which resisted the opposition of the native nobility and clergy to the foreigners. The settlers brought with them methods of cultivation which had already been used, particularly by the Carolingian emperors, for opening up and colonizing the Frankish lands, and which had proved to be an effective instrument in developing the powers of government. Now in the East these methods were improved, developed and used on a large scale, and often combined with the existing east European procedures, which they transformed and sometimes replaced. In this way the German element prevailed, the Slav inhabitants were Germanized, and a 'German East' was built up. But it is vitally important to distinguish between this 'German' or 'Germanized' East – confined to the territories of the small west Slav tribes, such as the Vagrians, the Obodrites, the Sorbs, the Wends and the Lusatians – and eastern Europe proper. The German or Germanized East exercised pressure on the lands between the German and the Russian borders, but the latter never lost the will and capacity to shape their own independent history.

The eastern frontier of the area of German domination was, of course, for a long time fluctuating. Down to the middle of the twelfth century it was marked by the territories ruled by the dynasties of Babenberg, Wettin and Ascania. After this time the colonizing movement spread out beyond the frontiers of the Empire and reached the mountainous country of Siebenbürgen in Hungary and the Baltic lands. In the south, Germans served under foreign rulers, but they were incorporated and privileged; in the north they established a strong dominion over a non-German population and connected it with the

Empire. In Silesia, Germans had no special status, but they put pressure on the Slavs simultaneously from above and from below.

The independent states of eastern Europe profited from this movement, which helped them to reach a level of civilization equal to that of the West. Some, such as fourteenth-century Bohemia, even surpassed it. In the occupied and Germanized territories of the 'German East', on the other hand, only a few remnants of the original Slav population survived, for instance in the so-called 'Lausitz', where a Slav idiom was preserved, although for centuries the people regarded themselves as German. Linguistic and political boundaries did not coincide in this area until very recent times. The early wars between Slavs and Germans were savagely fought on both sides; but the process of infiltration and cultural intermixture after these wars took place without force. Nevertheless Christian missions were often accompanied by force; it was, after all, St Bernard of Clairvaux who summoned the Germans to the crusade against the Wends in 1147. The Teutonic knights also used the idea of crusade as a justification for their pitiless attacks on the heathen Prussians; but these ideas came from western Europe. Nevertheless it is significant that a Germanizing melting process took place not only in areas subjected and conquered by force, where German marcher lords and other nobles ruled over both the native and the immigrant population – for example, the east march south of the river Danube from which Austria developed, or the marches of Meissen or Brandenburg – but even in such countries as Pomerania and Mecklenburg, where Slav princes and noblemen continued to rule although they were attached to the Empire by feudal bonds. The same is true of Silesia, which only became linked to the Empire in 1335 as a dependency of Bohemia, although it had become a country of German character long before that.

The chief agents of this melting process were the ruling dynasties, their nobility and the clergy. Gradually, by birth, by free decision, by custom or by marriage, the nationality of these groups changed. After that, a broad peasant class could be formed by the settling of immigrants and the assimilation of the native population. This brought the process of Germanization to a conclusion. On the other hand, German townsfolk and peasants were not able to retain their identity in a non-German environment, still less to give the Slav state a German character, in spite of their economic and cultural importance. In the Baltic lands the nobility gave them support, and the territorial princes were German.

The Czechs are justly proud of having preserved their national character, in spite of the fact that Bohemia and Moravia were members of the Empire, which more than once played a decisive part in shaping the course of events in Germany. Many factors helped the Czechs to maintain their national identity and gave them the strength to withstand German infiltration and assimilation. In the first place, German settlement was confined to the frontier regions of Bohemia and Moravia, where the Slavs themselves had not settled or had settled only in very small numbers. Thus considerable areas in the mountains on the borders of Bohemia – the Sudeten mountains, the Erzgebirge and the Bohemian Forest – became German-populated country as forests and swamps were opened up and cultivated. But the central area of Bohemia remained in the hands of the Czechs and Slavs, although in the cities and towns a German majority prevailed for a longer time and the countryside was infiltrated by islands of German language. Slavs and Germans in the towns were assimilated, and in a number of places the German citizens adopted the Czech language and nationality.

The German failure to assimilate the central region of Bohemia and Moravia was a decisive factor in checking and halting the process of Germanization in the independent Slav and Hungarian states further east. Nevertheless the Germanized territories in the East steadily gained momentum, power and weight in the later Middle Ages. The centre of gravity of the Empire shifted from West to East, as a result of German expansion. Not only did German territory increase by about a third as a result of the Germanization of the East, but bigger and more effective territorial states were created in the eastern areas, including Prussia, a union of the march of Brandenburg and the lands of the Teutonic knights, and Austria – the two powers which played a dominant part in German history down to the nineteenth century. Thereafter the centre of gravity moved back to the West under the influence of economic and social changes involving the whole of Europe. Nevertheless the significance of the German eastward movement in the Middle Ages is indicated by the fact that the two capitals of Berlin and Vienna were both situated in the newly colonized German East.

Apart from the expansion of German power and dominion, another basic feature was the assimilation of many peoples of Slav and Baltic descent. The tribes along the Elbe and other west Slav peoples lost their political identity as a result of German and Polish pressure, but their national substance was not destroyed. In the twelfth century a German eastward drive coincided with a Polish westward drive. Their rivalry was most clearly expressed in the field of ecclesiastical politics. The Poles founded the bishoprics of Włocławek, Lebus and Wollin-Cammin before the old German bishoprics of Brandenburg and Havelberg, which had perished in the Slav revolt of 983, were re-established, and before Henry the Lion, duke of Saxony and Bavaria from 1139 to 1180, began to found new ones. The archbishop of Magdeburg, Norbert of Xanten (d. 1134), famous as the founder of the Premonstratensian Order, was aware of the plans of the Poles, but failed to frustrate them at Rome. The Slavs on the Baltic Sea and on the Elbe and Oder, who preserved their pagan faith, were compelled to fight on two fronts. Not surprisingly they were unable to withstand this twofold pressure.

Politically, the defeat of Polish aspirations in this region was the result of the actions of German kings, princes and noblemen, and of the Teutonic Order; but socially it was the German peasants and settlers who Germanized the area in co-operation

32 Tympanum (*c.* 1200) from the Premonstratensian abbey of Strzelno; St Norbert and St Anne are represented as donors kneeling in front of the Virgin.

with German townsmen and German nobles. Living together with the native Slavs, these rural settlers assimilated them in process of time. By and large the German immigrants settled in areas of forest and swamp, which they cultivated, but they are also found in older settlements, where the islands of German immigrants became centres of the melting process. In the Baltic states, on the other hand, German infiltration was not successful, in spite of German political domination, because of the lack of German rural settlers. And Germanization was also frustrated in countries such as Bohemia and Poland, where the nobility and clergy resisted the movement; here the process of assimilation had a contrary effect and resulted in the absorption of the newcomers into the native population.

The Obodrites and Liutizi, the Pomeranians and Sorbs, the Slav tribes of Silesia, the Baltic Prussians, and last but not least the Slavs of the Alpine regions were not destroyed, but rather were integrated into a new mixed German-Slav population. They made a vital contribution to the formation of the 'Neustämme', or new ethnic groups, of eastern Germany. The strong

Slav admixture in the population of the eastern areas of the Empire – and later, as a new melting process got under way, in the population of western Germany – was one of the most far-reaching consequences of the political relations between eastern and western Europe during the Middle Ages. The east Germans are born of a mixture of native Slavs and German immigrants from the West, themselves the descendants of the older tribes of southern and western Germany, which were a mixture of pre-Germanic and other peoples, who came with the Romans into the areas around the Rhine and the Danube.

In the eyes of the Poles the knights of the Teutonic Order and their successors were invaders and aggressors, who pretended to be carrying out a Christian mission in order to conquer Slav territories and who ruthlessly used the power of the sword to plunder and subjugate peaceful people. Only united national resistance could overcome this inhuman onslaught. In this way both Poles and Germans came to see their history in the later Middle Ages as one of continuous national struggle. In reality, however, political relations between the German emperor and the Polish king were relatively peaceful during this period. Both powers were weakened by internal dissension and their interests had changed. When the Poles were again united, under Casimir the Great (1333–70), the main field of Polish political activity was in the East, where Galicia was occupied in the middle of the fourteenth century. Casimir's attitude towards the West was defensive, and he was even willing to sacrifice territory there in order to safeguard his rear. These were the circumstances in which Silesia, now divided into seventeen separate lordships under princes of the Silesian Piast dynasty, passed out of Polish hands and became part of Bohemia. The Silesian Piasts rendered homage to John of Bohemia, son of the German emperor, Henry VII, and the first ruler of the Luxembourg dynasty. And it is significant that it was the duke-doms of Upper Silesia where the Poles were in the majority that first accepted the feudal lordship of the Bohemian king, whereas the dukedoms of Lower Silesia with their strong

69

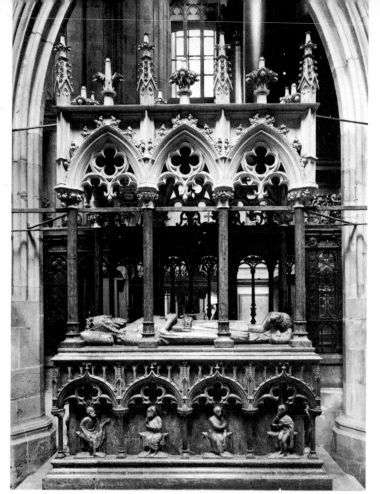

33 Tomb of
Casimir the Great
(1333–70)
of Poland in
Cracow cathedral
executed in 1376.

German minority remained subject to the Polish crown for a longer period. These facts do not suggest that Silesia was Germanized by force.

It was a Polish duke, Conrad of Masovia, who in 1225 invited the Teutonic Order and its grand master, Hermann of Salza, to come into his country, which had suffered heavily from the incursions of the pagan 'Pruzzi' or Prussians, a Baltic tribe of Lithuanian descent living between Poland and the Baltic Sea, from whom the name 'Prussia' is derived. Hermann of Salza succeeded in getting a privileged position from both emperor and pope, which made him for practical purposes independent of the territorial prince of Masovia. The Teutonic knights quickly conquered the Prussian lands, forced the Prussians to accept Christianity and freed the Masovians from the perilous attacks from the north. But this was only a beginning. The initial successes were exploited, after 1230, and a rapid expansion of the Order began. Towns were founded, German peasants settled on the land, and the knights soon built up a very progressive territorial state, independent of the Polish king; indeed, their militant, expansive state drew ahead of neighbouring Poland not only in administration and finance, but also in commerce and agriculture, and most of all in military power.

The knights had no hesitation about exploiting their preponderance. Though it is undeniable that the Teutonic Order disseminated western and Christian civilization in Prussia and Livonia, it is also undeniable that this was done by the sword rather than by preaching. Inevitably, the thrusting, aggressive policy of the Order produced a reaction, which came to a head after the death of the grand master, Winrich of Kniprode, in 1382. The dynastic union of Poland and Lithuania by the marriage between the Polish heiress, Hedwig, and Jagiello, the prince of Lithuania, in 1387, set up a barrier to further expansion.

34 Conrad of Masovia, his wife and two sons kneel in adoration before Christ on this patina (c. 1238).

It also resulted in the conversion of the Lithuanians, the last pagans in Europe, and with this conversion the missionary task of the Order ceased to make sense. At the same moment the ambiguity of its position became apparent. Enthusiasm for the crusade had disappeared; the influx of knights from the Empire declined; the citizens and other inhabitants of the Order state resented the heavy burden of clerical domination, which was becoming increasingly anachronistic. Hence the defeat of the Teutonic knights at Tannenberg in 1410 was a not unexpected military disaster, although the political situation still remained fluid. But the Poles definitely asserted their superiority in the peace treaty of Thorn (1466), when the territories of the Order were partitioned, the western part, with the port of Gdańsk (Danzig), passing to Poland. Half a century later the Teutonic state lost its clerical character when the grand master, Albrecht of Hohenzollern, became a vassal of the Polish king for the diminished territories which the Teutonic Order still retained.

The defeat and decay of the Teutonic Order was not the result of a national or racial conflict. The thirteen years' war, which ended in 1466, was waged by the Prussian Union, a federation of the cities of Gdańsk and Toruń (Thorn) with the rural gentry, who were laymen and not members of the Order. This was a German revolt against the territorial domination of the knights. Of course it is evident that the united strength of Poland and Lithuania was an important factor in weakening the position of the Order in the Baltic countries; unification with Lithuania made Poland a leading European power. But relations with the West played a secondary role in Polish policy at this stage. In the second half of the fifteenth century Poland's efforts were directed mainly against the rising power of Moscow in the East, although Jagiellons also ruled in Bohemia and Hungary.

It is undeniable, in summary, that the Teutonic knights pursued an aggressive policy. But it would be a mistake to judge the whole movement of German eastern colonization by this standard. The eastward movement of German settlers brought many Germans into Poland, but not according to a planned policy of expansion; their settlement was much more a consequence of measures of economic planning on the Slav side. Moreover, this movement did not harm the bulk of the Polish people. It was only in a few areas near the western frontier of Poland, especially in Silesia, that Germanization later took place; further east the German settlers, lacking any direct connection with their German homeland, were absorbed into the Polish nation after the close of the fifteenth century.

## THE RULE OF FOREIGN DYNASTIES AND THE RISE OF NATIONALISM

The fourth period in the political relations between East and West is characterized by the rule of foreign kings in Bohemia and Hungary and by a national reaction in the fifteenth century, especially the Hussite revolution in Bohemia, which quickly became an event of European significance.

Hungary had defended its leading position in the Danube valley in the first half of the thirteenth century. Its mighty nobility was privileged in 1222 by a charter similar to that obtained by the English barons in 1215. But the invasion of the Mongols and Tatars in 1241 disturbed the course of development both in Hungary and in Poland. After the Babenberg dynasty died out in Austria, in 1246, the Austrian nobility elected as successor the son of king Wenceslaus I of Bohemia. He was Přemysl Otakar II, who was elected king of Bohemia in 1253 after the death of his father. The Hungarians and the majority of the Polish dukes opposed this expansion of Bohemian power, particularly when, as a result of the defeats of king Béla IV of Hungary at the hands of the Mongols, Otakar also occupied the dukedoms of Styria, Carinthia and Carniola and united the territories of the Slovenes in Austria with his Bohemian kingdom. For a moment the territorial union of the south and west Slavs seemed a possibility. But Otakar's policy was not national and still less racial. Like his predecessors, he summoned German artisans, merchants, miners and settlers into his realm. The Czechs did not support him, and aided his rival, Rudolf of Habsburg, while the Polish princes formed a common Slav defensive alliance against the Germans.

Otakar's aim was the imperial German crown, which he hoped to win with the aid of the pope. Had he succeeded, Bohemia would no doubt have been linked more closely to Germany than it already was, and the character of the Empire would have undergone substantial changes under the rule of a Slav emperor. When the German princes elected Rudolf of Habsburg in 1273, Otakar had to defend his Austrian acquisitions against the new German king, who aspired to develop a strong territorial state in this area. The issue was decided in 1278 at the battle of the Marchfeld, north of Vienna, in which Otakar lost his life. The Habsburg dynasty was now free to pursue a policy of expansion beyond the frontiers of the Empire and the Danube area. The immediate result of the defeat of 1278 was a serious weakening of Czech power, and German and imperial influence in Bohemia and Moravia increased steadily. However, Wenceslaus II, Otakar II's son, was elected king of Poland in 1300, and in the following year his son was crowned king of Hungary, on the death of Andrew III, last representative of the Arpad dynasty. Thus Bohemia, Poland and Hungary were united for a short time, but only by dynastic union.

This did not last long. With the murder of Wenceslaus III in 1306 the old Czech royal family of the Přemyslids died out. This event released the Polish Piasts from the continuous pressure of the Přemyslid kings and secured the complete independence of their country. It also set up rivalry for the thrones of Bohemia and of Hungary. Both the Habsburg dynasty and the Wittelsbach dukes of Bavaria competed for the crowns of St Wenceslaus and St Stephen. Neither succeeded. With the help of the pope, Charles Robert, a scion of the French Angevin dynasty, was elected king of Hungary in 1308. This foreign dynasty preserved the traditions of Hungarian independence and blocked the growing German influence. In Bohemia Přemyslid rule was followed by that of the western house of Luxembourg, which also was strongly influenced by French connections and

The last Přemyslids, Otakar II, king of Bohemia, Wenceslaus II, king of Bohemia and Poland, and Wenceslaus III, king of Bohemia, Poland and Hungary; from the fourteenth-century manuscript, *Chronicon Aulae Regiae*.

attitudes. John of Luxembourg, who succeeded in 1310, was the son of the emperor, Henry VII, and both he and his son Charles IV, German emperor and king of Bohemia, followed the French style of education and a French way of life during the whole of their careers. Working in co-operation with the Teutonic Order, they became very dangerous rivals of Poland. At the end of the fourteenth century they also won the Hungarian crown.

These developments in Bohemia and Hungary, taken together with the rise of Moscow and the invasion of the Balkans by the Turks, marked a climax in the history of eastern and central Europe. The reign of Charles IV was both a turning-point in German history and a period of extraordinary progress in the Bohemian lands. Prague became the capital of the Empire and Bohemia played a leading part both in politics and

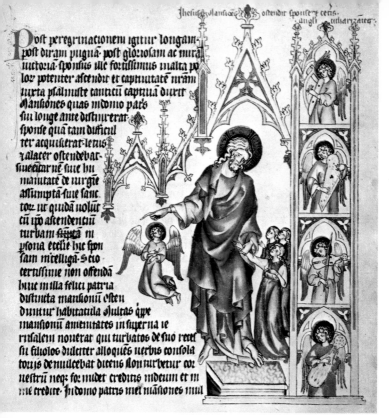

36 'Christ leading the souls of the righteous into heaven' from Abbess Cunegon Passionary, a Bohemia manuscript illuminate *c.* 1320.

37 Charles IV (1316–78), detail of a painting attributed to Master Theodoric (*c.* 1370).

in culture. The foundation of the first university of central Europe in Prague by Charles IV in 1348 indicates the momentum Bohemia had gained under his rule. Shortly afterwards universities were established, more or less simultaneously, at Cracow in Poland, at Pécs (Fünfkirchen) in Hungary, and at Vienna in Austria.

It is true that this flourishing civilization and the close contacts with the West, particularly with Germany, had to be paid for by stricter dependence on the Empire, which threatened loss of independence and of liberty of decision. On the other hand, the Bohemian lands were organized ecclesiastically in 1344 as a single independent archbishopric; the kingdom of Bohemia now had its own autonomous territorial church. After having occupied the whole of Lausitz, Charles acquired the march of Brandenburg for his son Sigismund; the Ascanian and Wittelsbach dynasties had already made this territory a strong German bulwark, menacing the independence of Poland. The emperor also arranged a dynastic marriage between his son and Mary, the heiress of Hungary, daughter of the last Angevin king of that country, Louis the Great, who

38 Wenceslaus IV (1361–1419) in his coronation robes; from a late fourteenth-century miniature.

died in 1382. Thus the idea of a union of Bohemia and Hungary, going back to the time of Otakar II, was revived.

The Angevins had come to Hungary from Italy, and at their courts at Buda or Wissegrad there was a flourishing French and Italian civilization with elements of early Renaissance culture. Charles Robert co-operated with the Polish king very closely and married Elisabeth of Poland, daughter of Władisław Łokietek, in 1320. Louis the Great, son of Charles Robert, had to face the hostility of the biggest commercial power in the region, the republic of Venice; but he was able to reoccupy Dalmatia in 1358. After 1370 he was also king of Poland following the death of the last of the Piasts. But he had no sons, and his heritage fell to his daughters. The marriage of Hedwig with William of Habsburg was intended as a first step towards union between Hungary and Austria. But after Louis the Great's death a national reaction intervened and the plan came to nothing. As in Poland and a little later in Bohemia, a national revolution swept away the foreign influences which had prevailed under the foreign kings.

Meanwhile Serbia had made great progress under the rule of Stefan Dušan, the greatest monarch of his time, who planned to build a Serbian empire, which should replace the Byzantine empire of the Paleologues in the Balkans. Dušan was named 'imperator Daciae et Romaniae'. But Serbian power and independence collapsed completely on the battlefield of Kossovo in 1389 under the blows of the Turkish general, Murad I. Bulgaria also was conquered and occupied by the Turks after the destruction of its capital Trnovo in 1393, and national life and civilization were extinguished in the Balkans for half a millennium.

The fifteenth century in eastern Europe was characterized by the rise of national kingdoms in Bohemia and Hungary and by expansion on the eastern frontiers of the united Polish-Lithuanian state by the Jagiellonian kings. It was Sigismund, son of Charles IV and ruler of Germany since the forced abdication of his brother Wenceslaus (or Vaclav) in 1400, who

39 Louis the Great (1326–82) of Hungary and his court; from the Hungarian *Picture Chronicle*.

lit the spark which kindled the nationalism of Bohemia. By summoning the Czech reformer Jan Hus before the Council of Constance (1414–18), and condemning him to death because he refused to renounce his religious views, Sigismund provoked a national reaction in the Bohemian lands. The Hussite revolution was the first social movement in Europe with an explicit will to change the whole order of society. It was also a rebellion for Czech independence. Against this revolt, backed by the estates of Bohemia, the idea of crusade, invoked by pope and emperor, proved ineffective. The Hussites under the military leadership of Jan Žižka and Procop launched attacks on the neighbouring countries; but all German counter-attacks were defeated, and the Taborites became a military power. The Poles also had already strongly resisted the concept of imperial supremacy at the Council of Constance.

Meanwhile Bohemia was suffering from the ravages of war, and the Council of Basel, which convened in 1431, made peace

40 A priest carries a monstrance in front of the blind Taborite leader Jan Žižka on a horse; from the late fifteenth-century Jena Codex.

with the moderate wing of the Hussites. Both sides agreed in 1433 to sign the so-called Compacts of Prague, which approved the minimal demands of the Czech reform movement, and the radical Hussite wing of the movement was defeated in 1434 at the battle of Lipany. The emperor Sigismund was then acknowledged as king of Bohemia. Finally, therefore, he succeeded in uniting the crowns of the Empire, Bohemia and Hungary. But this success was precarious and short-lived. When Sigismund died in 1437 without a son, he transferred his three kingdoms to Albrecht of Habsburg, the husband of his daughter Elisabeth. But Albrecht also died in 1439, leaving a posthumous son, Ladislaus, as heir to Bohemia and Hungary. His claims were never effective; Bohemia and Hungary were riddled with civil war, and when Ladislaus died in 1457, national kings were elected in both realms, for the representatives of the estates were

41 Above left, marble relief of Matthias Corvinus (1440–90), king of Hungary; by a Lombard master.

42 Above right, Casimir IV (1427–92), king of Poland; detail from his marble tomb in Cracow cathedral, constructed by Veit Stoss at the end of the fifteenth century.

43 George of Poděbrad (1420–71), king of Bohemia, who lost his throne to Matthias in 1466; from an early sixteenth-century manuscript.

very strong and effective in both countries. George of Podě-brad, a Czech nobleman of Utraquistic confession, became king of Bohemia; Matthias Corvinus, son of the Hungarian national hero, John Hunyadi, was elected king of Hungary. But Casimir Jagiello of Poland, husband of Albrecht II's daughter, Elisabeth, also laid claim to the crowns, as did the Habsburg emperor, Frederick III. Eventually, but not until the next century, the Habsburg claims proved successful, and Hungary and Bohemia passed under Habsburg rule, which lasted until 1918.

The Slav nations of eastern Europe, no less than the Romano-Germanic nations of the West, are constituent elements of European society and civilization. The political relations between western and eastern Europe in the Middle Ages, under-pinned and supported by Christian missions and ecclesiastical organization, as well as by trade, commerce, urban develop-ment, law and science, brought both parts into contact, inaugurated a process of assimilation, and introduced similar standards in both regions. These relations, it is true, were often hostile; many wars and much fighting took place; but the traditional emphasis of historians on wars and assassinations too easily obscures the fact that most of the time relations were peaceful. To a large extent political relations were made up of dynastic marriages between the ruling families, of legations of all kinds, of the exchange of gifts and privileges, of treaties, agreements, conferences and meetings, and they assumed a wide variety of forms of association, not all of them implying subjection. In all these ways the tribes and nations of eastern Europe were not only able to establish more or less independent states of their own, but also became fully fledged members of the Christian society of medieval Europe.

# III THE RELIGIOUS PROBLEMS
*Ferdinand Seibt*

## THE SPREAD AND ORGANIZATION OF CHRISTIANITY:
## THE MONKS

The religious development of medieval Europe cannot be understood without reference to geographical factors. First of all there are the links between north and south: in the south, in Italy, in southern France and in Spain, something of the civilization of antiquity survived, preserving ancient traditions on which the barbarian north lived until Carolingian civilization gave it 'a new breath of life'. From the south, from Rome, the papacy gradually organized the framework of Christianity, its expansion, and its own position in the Christian world. The name of the ancient capital came to be linked in a unique way in Latin Christendom with the sacred memories of the apostles Peter and Paul: *Roma aeterna – Roma sacra*.

Another link with ancient civilization was less strong but nevertheless significant: Byzantium, the second centre of Christianity and the home of Roman imperial tradition handed down in unbroken succession since Constantine the Great. It was not until the beginning of the ninth century that a western ruler, Charlemagne, was recognized as an equal by the Byzantine emperors; it was not until the end of the tenth century that it became clear where in this dual Europe the boundaries of the Roman church and thus of the tradition of Latin civilization would be drawn in relation to those of the Greco-Byzantine church. The papacy succeeded where Charlemagne and his successors failed: it unified the whole of Latin Christianity into the 'occident', from the Mediterranean to the Atlantic, from the Bug to Gibraltar. Southern Italy, Spain, England and Scandinavia, islands and peninsulas on the periphery of this civilization, remained outside the Frankish-German Empire but

44 Christ blesses the German emperor Otto II (955–83) and his Byzantine wife Theophano; their marriage was arranged by Otto's father to improve political relations between East and West. From a late tenth-century ivory relief.

recognized the ecclesiastical authority of the Roman popes. In the south the frontier between the Roman and the Byzantine church roughly followed the line drawn by the emperor Diocletian when he divided the Roman empire in AD 285. In the north it cut through the second big ethnic group which after the Germans became part of the European community: the Slavs. The west Slavs became 'Latin', the east Slavs, the Bulgarians and the Serbs became 'Greek'.

The Tatar invasion in the thirteenth century and the expansion of the Turks in the fourteenth and fifteenth centuries put an end, for hundreds of years, to the independent political existence of these east Slav peoples, as well as destroying the Byzantine empire. Western Europe on the other hand was affected by Islamic expansion only for a short period at its periphery in southern Italy and in Spain; later it even benefited from contacts with the Arabs because the latter had been more successful than the inhabitants of western Europe in assimilating and maintaining Hellenistic traditions. But even after the schism between

Latin and Greek Christianity in 1054, a schism which has lasted to this day, contacts with Byzantium continued to influence the intellectual life of the West.

Nevertheless the connections with Byzantium were secondary. For the West it soon became more important to reduce the tensions and differences among the countries of western Europe, influenced by the ancient world and favoured economically by natural advantages, and the territories east of the Elbe, whose development in the beginning failed, in Gieysztor's words, to keep in step with 'the rhythm of the history of Christian Europe'.

In this process a decisive part was played by the Frankish empire. The Franks had adopted the Catholic faith at the turn of the sixth century. But it was only in the territories within the boundaries of ancient Rome that Christianity was really vigorous, most strongly of all in southern Gaul, and it was not until the seventh century that Catholic missions from the West reached the eastern regions of the Frankish empire. The organization of the church was based on a monastic culture which had survived the ruin of the ancient world and maintained a foothold in southern Gaul, but which found its safest

45 Early sixth-century sarcophagus from Castelnau-de-Guers, France. Christ (centre), St Peter (right) and St Paul (left) stand between panels decorated with an ornamental motif of wine leaves and grapes.

refuge in distant Ireland. It was from Ireland that, in the seventh century, itinerant monks set out on missions which took them as far afield as Switzerland, Bavaria, central Germany and Bobbio in northern Italy. In the eighth century Anglo-Saxon Benedictines laid the foundations for the organization of the church between the Rhine and the Elbe. The outstanding figure was Winfrid, or Boniface, as he was later called. The episcopal system of Germany today is still based essentially on the divisions he organized, and Irish and Anglo-Saxon missionaries are still revered by German Catholics as the founders of their church.

The itinerant monks from Ireland and England had travelled eastward in the seventh and eighth centuries because it was there that the nearest heathen or barely Christianized sphere of action was found. In the same way and for the same reason, a century later, monasteries in the east of the Frankish empire also began to carry Christianity eastward. Boniface himself had been concerned with the conversion of the Slavs who lived within the boundaries of the Carolingian empire in eastern Franconia and Thuringia.

But Christianity meanwhile had acquired political overtones, largely as a consequence of the conditions in which it was adopted. Papal claims notwithstanding, the Catholic church in the Frankish lands had, in the course of the eighth century, become the 'imperial church' of the Frankish empire. The Merovingian and Carolingian kings claimed its allegiance; the aristocracy had laid its hands on it, providing bishops and abbots, founding monasteries for its kin, and seeking to adapt Christian values to its own social ideas. Christianity had thus become in many respects a political creed, and as such it played an important part in the expansion of the Frankish empire.

This was seen in the long conflict between Charlemagne and the Saxons which lasted over thirty years, from 772 to 804. As a means of subjugating the Saxons, they were forced to become Christians. Not that evangelization was always politically
motivated. Frankish missions also spread beyond the eastern

46 Cyril and Methodius composing the 'Cyrillic' script; detail of a manuscript page from the fifteenth-century Radziwill Chronicle.

boundaries of the Empire without direct political pressure. It was in this peaceful way that the Christian message reached the first west Slav empire of which we have specific knowledge, the Great Moravian empire of the ninth century which is reputed to have embraced a primitive form of Christianity (*rudis adhuc christianitas*) by 852. But at this point, it would seem, the political factor came into play. Frankish, Greek and Italian missionaries all suddenly appeared in Moravia, seeking to organize the church according to their own rites and link it with their own organizations. The Moravians, jealous of their independence, were particularly suspicious of Frankish pressure, and so their prince, Rastislav, turned to Byzantium, asking for advisers to organize his church. This was the origin of the famous mission of the brothers Cyril (d. 869) and Methodius (d. 885). The two brothers, who had been in Moravia since 863, came from Salonika and were familiar with the Slav language, as well as outstanding representatives of Byzantine intellectual life. By translating the liturgical texts into the Slavonic language and even perhaps by inventing the 'Cyrillic' script, they made the Christian scriptures accessible to the Bulgarians and eventually to the Russians. In Moravia

87

47 St Boniface baptizes the heathens; detail of a manuscript page from the eleventh-century Fulda Sacramentary.

their efforts were unsuccessful, although traces of their influence survived in Bohemia until the eleventh century and possibly for a shorter time in southern Poland. But papal suspicion, Frankish policy and the claims of the Bavarian episcopacy all conspired to bring their work in Moravia to nothing, and after Methodius' death priests of the Slavonic liturgy were expelled from Moravia.

The popes for a time had countenanced the Slavonic liturgy and had even appointed Methodius as archbishop of Moravia and Pannonia. This was partly an attempt to pursue a policy in eastern Europe independent of the Frankish empire, partly an attempt to offset the influence of Constantinople and secure the papacy's hold over the Balkan Slavs. A Moravian archdiocese would have strengthened the contacts with central Europe which Methodius again tried to consolidate by a journey in 881–82. Moreover, by uniting the west Slavs and the south Slavs the establishment of such a diocese would have affected the whole future cultural and political development of Europe. But such possibilities were not destined to bear fruit. The forced submission of Rastislav to Louis the German in 864 and the machinations of the Frankish clergy with their 'urge for cultural domination and political control' (Obolensky), destroyed the auspicious beginnings. Finally, the invasions of the Magyars changed the whole situation. In 906 the Moravian empire fell victim to the Magyar invaders, and from that time forward the spread of Christianity in central Europe was again in the hands of the east Franks who by now had broken loose from the Carolingian empire and were forming an independent kingdom under a new dynasty – the *regnum Teutonicorum*, or the kingdom of Germany.

48 A silver pectoral crucifix, cast in the March valley in the ninth century.

49 A priest or saint at prayer on a ninth-century amulet found at Mikulčice in Moravia.

Henceforward, it seems to anyone looking back over the course of events in retrospect, missionary activity and political subjugation were all too often inextricably linked. This is certainly not entirely false; but there are other considerations which make it clear that the spread of Christianity was not simply a result of military force and political pressure.

First of all, although we know little about the heathen cults of northern Europe, it seems evident that Christianity, whether among the Saxons in the eighth century or the Poles in the tenth century, was superior to them all. This superiority is immediately visible in the external forms of religion; for example, churches built of stone, a form of construction hitherto unknown, increased rapidly in Moravia and around 900 in Bohemia; from there half a century later they reached southern Poland and shortly afterwards northern Poland. In addition there was the splendour of the liturgy and the solid substructure of a written religion. This cultural superiority alone is likely to have contributed much to the spread of Christianity.

50 The celebration of mass;
from an Ottonian
ivory book-cover.

51 Foundations of the ninth-century church at Sady in Moravia; the cross-shaped ground-plan suggests Carolingian influence.

Secondly, although conversion was often superficial, Christianity had far-reaching consequences precisely because of its political aspects. As Gieysztor has said, new 'civil rights' were acquired by peoples who entered the *imperium christianum*. Converted heathen princes were treated as equals in international relations; Christianity assured their principalities universal recognition and thus also some degree of independence. As the organization of the western church proceeded in the eighth and ninth centuries, the archbishoprics that were set up reflected political boundaries and assured some measure of local autonomy in relations with the papacy; and it is significant that the coincidence between political frontiers and ecclesiastical boundaries was more marked in eastern and central Europe than in the regions to which Christianity had spread earlier.

Finally, it was even easier in the East for the ecclesiastical and the temporal authorities to work together than it was in the West. In general Christianity spread 'from above'; that is to say, the ruler and his followers – the prince 'cum nobilibus viris fidelibus et cum omni populo terrae', as the pope expressed it in 880 with reference to the Moravian empire – accepted the new faith and enforced it from the top of the social hierarchy downwards. As in the case of the Germans several centuries earlier, the introduction of Christianity among the Slavs coincided with a process of political centralization. In places where this process had already reached a certain degree of stability the    91 missions assisted it; elsewhere they complicated it by adding ideological differences to the political conflict. Established kingdoms derived benefit from Christianization, which strengthened the position of the ruler and gave him international legitimization, and in case of need might even enable him to obtain assistance from neighbouring Christian princes. But where the central government was weak or as yet non-existent, the Christian missions only progressed slowly and, if there was a return to paganism, used apostasy as a pretext for recourse to force. This happened in the case of the Friesian and Saxon tribes in the eighth century; it also happened two hundred years later in the case of many of the small Slav tribes between the Elbe and Oder. The same arguments were advanced to legitimize the use of force by the Poles during the Pomeranian mission, by the Teutonic Order in heathen Prussia, by Spain during the Reconquista and by the English in Wales.

The course of events between the Elbe and the Oder from the tenth to the twelfth century shows how the different lines of development were connected. For unknown reasons the formation of large tribes was further advanced in the north of this region than in the centre; in the south it was still in its early stages. The Christian missions affected the political situation correspondingly. Setbacks notwithstanding, Slav dynasties survived in the northern parts of the Slav settlement area until modern times, even though they had meanwhile become Germanized and linked politically with the Empire. With compromises, some even survived the vicious, aggressive 'Wendish crusade' of 1147 about which even contemporaries were critical. In the central area, on the other hand, the native dynasty disappeared in 1150 after a dramatic conflict with the heathen nobility, in its struggle with which it had repeatedly been assisted by its Saxon neighbours. In the southern area no single territorial unit seems to have existed before missionary work began. As early as the tenth century the area broke up into a German sphere of interest in the west, the future march of Meissen, while

Poland and Bohemia struggled for control of the eastern region (the future Upper and Lower Lausitz).

In Bohemia, Poland and Hungary conditions were less complicated. Here Christianization assisted the centralizing efforts of the Přemyslid, Piast and Arpad dynasties. Bohemia, which was two generations ahead of the other two countries, retained closer links with its German neighbours; but that did not affect its internal development. Poland and Hungary achieved an independent position by the year 1000. But it is anachronous to describe these events in terms of the modern sovereign state. Mieszko I of Poland, baptized in 966, after his marriage to a Christian princess from Bohemia, resisted claims for tribute from the German kings. But his son Boleslav I was made *frater et cooperator imperii* by Otto III in 1000, and even Boleslav's immediate successors were not averse to the idea of co-operation, not as satellites or dependants but as active participants in an imperial plan for establishing harmony in central and eastern Europe. It was Otto's successor, Henry II,

52 Henry II receives the blessing of Christ in glory; miniature from a sacramentary produced for the emperor – probably in Regensburg between 1002 and 1014.

who abandoned this plan. By entering into an anti-Polish alliance with the heathen Liutizi, one of the Slav peoples on the Elbe, Henry (as H. Ludat has said) opened a 'gulf between western and eastern central Europe' which brought the era of co-operation to an end and set Germany and Poland on separate and usually hostile paths.

The organization of the church in east central Europe was undertaken and encouraged by the imperial church under the three Ottonian emperors in the second half of the tenth century, though in the last phase Bohemia also began to play an active role in missionary work. The organization covered the whole area east of the Elbe from Denmark to Hungary in a large semicircle. Originally the archbishoprics of Bremen (founded in 834), Magdeburg (founded in 968) and Salzburg (founded in 805) were intended as missionary centres, but the establishment of Gniezno in Poland and Gran in Hungary in the year 1000 put an end to further German missionary expansion to the east and south-east, just as later the Scandinavian archbishopric of Lund (founded in 1104) put an end to the ambitions of Bremen in the north. And in choosing personnel for the new archbishoprics the nascent churches of the East also soon showed their independence of the West.

In the early period immediately following its foundation in 805, the missionary work of Salzburg was concentrated on the Slavs of the Alpine valleys and the conversion of the Avars. Later, when the Christianization of the Moravian empire took place, Salzburg no longer had the field to itself. Apart from the Italian and Byzantine competition to which we have already referred, its own suffragan bishoprics were also active, Passau probably to a lesser extent than the important mission centre of Regensburg. The archbishopric of Magdeburg was founded by the emperor Otto I with ambitious objectives. Its first archbishop, Adalbert of Weissenburg from the monastery of St Maximin near Trier, had previously been active as a missionary bishop in the principality of Kiev. But when Kiev opted for Greek Christianity, Otto I still saw great tasks to be accom-

53 The nave of the Romanesque church of St George in Prague dates from after 1142 – the original church was burnt down.

plished among the Slav tribes between the Elbe and the Bug, and these were confided to Magdeburg. For this reason the archbishops of Magdeburg did not accept the independent organization of the Polish church without fierce opposition. Byzantine influence lasted longest in the south-east, in Hungary. At one stage there were attempts to revive Methodius' old archdiocese, but finally a new Hungarian archbishopric of Gran was established, and freed itself completely from the influence of Salzburg.

As had been the case in the West in the seventh and eighth centuries, it was the monks who brought Christianity to the East. Up to the year 1000 the ecclesiastical organization depended largely on them. The Benedictine abbey of St Emmeram at Regensburg, the seat of the bishopric until 975, was one of the most important training centres for the Slav mission. In particular, it participated actively in the establishment, organization and training of the clergy of the bishopric of Prague, which only became an independent diocese in 973. The oldest convent in Bohemia, the community of St George

95

ANGELVS ECELO MISSVS RESIDENSQ: SEPVLCHRO. SVRREXISSE DM VOTIS RESERAT MVLIERVM. VT PERQVAS MISTRVM CEPIT MORS LIVIDA MVNDVM NVNC PER EAS VITAE CLARESCANT GAVDIA RITE

54 Holy Women at the Sepulchre; manuscript page from the Vyšehrad Codex (*c.* 1086) whi may have been produced for the coronation of Vratislav II as first king of Bohemia.

on the Hradčany in Prague, an order for gentlewomen, was founded in 972 by a Přemyslid princess educated at Regensburg. Monks from Bavarian Niederaltaich on the Danube founded what is probably the oldest Benedictine monastery in Bohemia, at Ostrov on the Beraun. There is also evidence that the monk Boso from St Emmeram, later the first bishop of Merseburg, made serious attempts to do missionary work among the Slavs and acquired the necessary linguistic training; indeed we know from surviving manuscripts that languages were taught at St Emmeram. But St Emmeram, although the most important, was only one missionary centre. Other Benedictine foundations, such as Reichenau on Lake Constance or Korvey in Saxony also provided abbots, bishops and monks, supplied manuscripts and brought the worship of their own particular saints – St Emmeram, St George, St Vitus – to the new regions.

At a time when the monasteries were still the leading element in the church, great efforts were made to carry to eastern and central Europe the reform movement which was spreading across Europe from the monasteries of Gorze in Lorraine and Cluny in Burgundy and from northern Italy. This reform movement aimed at securing independence for the churches and

55 Murder of St Wenceslaus in 935; manuscript page from a codex illuminated around 1000.

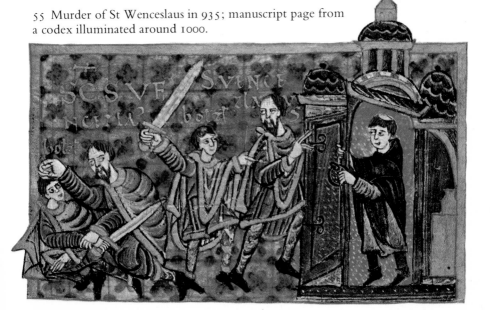

at inculcating a more vital Christian spirit reflecting the ideals of Benedictine monasticism. It was also influenced via Italy by Byzantine monastic culture. It gained the support of the emperor Otto III, who seems to have tried to combine Roman imperial traditions with the office of a vicar of Christ, and for some years it seemed as though central Europe might be reshaped in greater understanding of the Christian heritage by an alliance between the pope, the emperor and the monastic reform movement. The emperor's interest in the recently Christianized territories of eastern Europe was particularly significant in this connection.

Otto III himself was close to the eremitical movements of Italy. The second bishop of Prague, Adalbert, and his followers and friends were also closely connected with this movement and with the reform monastery of San Alessio in Rome. Adalbert himself belonged to the princely family of the Slavnikids, the Bohemian dynasty which competed for dominion with the Přemyslids. This dynasty maintained good relations both with the German imperial house and with Poland, until in 995 it was almost completely exterminated by a Přemyslid massacre. The history of the Přemyslids had been marred before by similar incidents, as was the early history of several other European dynasties. In 935, for example, the Christian duke Wenceslaus had been murdered by his brother, and was revered thereafter as a holy martyr for the church. Such incidents show the way in which political opposition and heathen opposition – and also resistance to German influence – coalesced. Two generations later Adalbert found the Christian spirit of the leaders of Bohemia still seriously threatened by paganism. In 992 he assigned monks from San Alessio to a Benedictine monastery at Brevnov near Prague, hoping with their help to raise the standard of Christianity in Bohemia. But he himself preferred life at the imperial court or the asceticism of his Italian monastery.

In Poland also, the first bishopric set up at Poznań in 966 was a monastic missionary bishopric, staffed in all probability by monks from Liège, from where the first bishop is thought to have come. In 1001 five hermits from Pereum near Ravenna joined the Polish mission and quickly suffered martyrdom. Abbot Odilo of Cluny was one of the advisers of the young emperor and a friend of Adalbert of Prague and his circle. In 996 Adalbert founded a second Benedictine monastery in Poland which he put in charge of an abbot with the Burgundian name, Ascherich (or Anastasius). Later this abbot led the Benedictines to Hungary and became the first Hungarian archbishop, while the Polish see of Gniezno was given to Adalbert's brother, Gaudentius.

In 997 Adalbert died the death of a martyr during a mission to the Baltic and was canonized by the pope. Barefooted, the emperor made a pilgrimage to Adalbert's grave at Gniezno, where he founded a new archbishopric for Poland. Gniezno, Gran, Prague, Pereum and other important centres of the reform movement made Adalbert their patron saint; half a dozen biographies glorified his death. It seemed like the beginning of a new era of reconciliation between Germans and Slavs, but instead Adalbert's life became the symbol of the failure of such plans. The death of Otto III in 1002, followed soon afterward by the death of his friend and teacher, pope Sylvester II, marked the end of his policies. With the succession of the emperor Henry II, the political situation in eastern Europe changed and the Christianization of society proceeded along lines different from those planned by Otto III.

56 The landing of St Adalbert in Prussia; relief from the twelfth-century bronze doors of Gniezno cathedral.

When, in the middle of the eleventh century, the Cluniacs were once again able to win the support of the temporal rulers, to reform the papacy and to put reformers on the papal throne, the territories east of the Elbe and in Hungary, which had recently been converted to Christianity, were hardly affected. At that time there were barely two dozen Benedictine monasteries in that part of the world and although most of them were in touch with the monastic reform movement in the West it is obvious that they could not exercise anything like the same influence as the 2,000 or more Cluniac monasteries of western Europe. Occasionally the popes turned for support to the rulers of Hungary and Poland, and their search for allies extended even as far as Kiev; but their efforts were purely political and did not have much impact on the position of the churches in the East. The coronation of Boleslav II as king of Poland in 1076 was not the result of the pope's support but rather a manifestation of Polish independence. Here and even more in Bohemia, which was raised to the rank of a kingdom by the emperor Henry IV in 1085, the temporal rulers controlled the church, appointed bishops and resisted the demands of the reformers, particularly of the Benedictine abbots, for independence. The spirit of Cluniac reform made no headway in eastern Europe.

## CHURCH AND STATE: THE BISHOPS

Nevertheless in the course of the twelfth century, the church in Poland, Bohemia and Hungary underwent an important maturing process which enabled it to take up the struggle for independence after a delay of over a hundred years. It was not until the second half of the eleventh century, after political confusion and heathen reaction, that the organization of the church in these countries was finally consolidated. In the process the monks were gradually relieved of the burden of general church work, although the religious Orders continued to play an important part in cultural and economic development. The monks were replaced by secular clergy. The bishops were for

100

57 Foundations of an early 'proprietary church' near Alfeld in Germany (seventh century) ▶

the most part no longer Benedictines, but were priests trained in the residential establishments for the clergy which had grown up alongside the cathedrals and other important churches: the collegiate chapters.

The importance of this form of organization of the secular clergy has long been underestimated because it lacked the compactness of the monastic Orders. But there is plenty of evidence that it was effective. In Bohemia in the middle of the eleventh century the collegiate chapters regularly provided the church leadership and were among the most respected institutions. By the end of the twelfth century there were at least fifty such chapters in Poland, twice as many as the total number of Benedictine and Cistercian abbeys at that time (J. Koczowski). These chapters were of particular importance for the ecclesiastical and intellectual life of the period because they trained the clergy and kept them together under episcopal supervision before they found other important tasks, such as parochial work.

In the eleventh and even in the twelfth century the parochial system was only just beginning to take shape. There was only a sparse network of parish churches, attached in most cases to the local centres of administration as 'castle parsonages', or founded as 'proprietary churches' on the estates of a rich lord. And just

as the 'proprietary churches' were dependent on the princes or great lords, so also the episcopal sees were centred on the estates of the ruling dynasty, with the result that the bishops depended on the ruler almost like officials. As late as 1182 the Bohemian duke described the bishop of Prague in a legal dispute quite simply as his court chaplain. This was very different from the princely rank the German bishops had occupied since the tenth century, and still more from the independent position the episcopacy had secured in the West after the investiture conflicts at the close of the eleventh century.

Gradually, however, the episcopacy in eastern Europe made use of changing political conditions to improve its position. In Poland in the late twelfth and thirteenth centuries the Piast dynasty had split into numerous lines so that the church, fairly free from pressure by the princes, became the most important element of national unity. In the Bohemian territories similar conditions helped the bishops of Olomouc (Olmütz) in Moravia to acquire a greater degree of independence than the bishops of Prague achieved at the sovereign's residence. In Hungary conditions were less favourable. Although the Hungarian bishops continued, in spite of the Cluniacs' reforming efforts, to supervise and control the monasteries, they themselves remained dependent on the monarchy longer than their Polish and Bohemian colleagues.

The rise of the episcopacy was assisted by the papacy. After the investiture controversies the papacy reshaped and extended its claims and proclaimed that the law of the church, the so-called canon law, was universally valid and superior to temporal law. In eastern Europe such claims were even further removed from reality than in the West. In western Europe the church was generally older than the secular administration; already in earlier centuries it had acquired lands and seigniorial rights which were more or less the equivalent of great independent lordships. During the investiture contest these so-called 'immunities' were freed from all temporal supervision, and the great ecclesiastics, bishops and abbots, became the peers and equals of the great secular magnates, holding their lands like them by feudal law. In eastern Europe, on the other hand, the church had only spread after the temporal authority was established. The bishoprics were seen as foundations of the princes and treated accordingly; the administration of church property and the appointment of bishops and priests were wholly or largely – and certainly according to the prevalent ideas quite legitimately – in the hands of the founders and their successors. The church was not self-governing, nor did it have courts of its own for the clergy. In this part of Europe, therefore, the rise of canon law in the twelfth century with its claims to supremacy and its concept of the church as a free, self-governing body, was an important factor in bringing about the gradual disappearance of the old forms of dependence.

A further factor in the rise of the episcopacy was the separation of the clergy from the rest of society and its development into a separate social group or estate, with its own organization and ideology. The collegiate chapters, with their ideal of an ascetic life on the lines of the Benedictine reformers, pointed the way. But it was the enforcement of celibacy that produced the most important social results. Through celibacy even the lesser clergy broke their family ties and were brought completely under the ecclesiastical hierarchy. But to maintain this division in a church which also saw itself as the community of all the faithful, was a difficult task. The inherent conflict between the clerical way of life and that of the laity could only be resolved if and when the clergy assumed special duties, which justified its privileged position.

One such duty – looking after the welfare of laity – made the secular clergy into a powerful group in medieval society, and it was by discharging this duty that they finally overtook the monks, who had led the way in the Christianization of eastern Europe. But the change was slow and gradual. The organization of parishes, the training of a parish clergy, and the idea of ministering to the laity, were not yet sufficiently far advanced in central and eastern Europe in the eleventh and twelfth

centuries to obviate the need for 'canons regular' – that is, secular clergy living together like monks in convents. Thus the monastic model provided a framework for the secular clergy as it began its pastoral work. The new houses of secular clergy often developed from the older collegiate chapters, until finally they were organized as the Order of Augustinian canons. The Augustinian canons played an important role in the church life of south Germany and Austria in the eleventh and twelfth centuries, but they are not found in eastern Europe at this period. Here it was the Premonstratensians, a similar Order but with a better organization, that made an impact. The spread of the Premonstratensians into the territories east of the Elbe began after their founder, Norbert of Xanten, reorganized the archbishopric of Magdeburg, and by the thirteenth century they were playing an important part in the East, two or three generations after their flowering in the West.

59 Ruins of the thirteenth-century Premonstratensian church of Zsambék in Hungary.

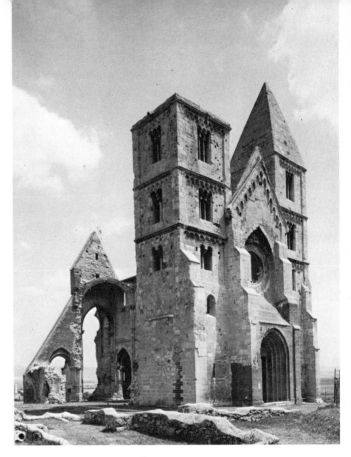

60 Below left, detail of a tympanum representing David playing the harp; from a nun's church at Trzebnica (first half of the thirteenth century).

61 Left, south window of the chapter-house of the abbey of Wachok (first half of the thirteenth century).

105

Together with the Cistercians, the Premonstratensians were leaders in land reclamation and colonization, a task which not only gave them an opportunity of developing their own settlements, but also contributed greatly to the cultural development of eastern Europe. Cistercians and Premonstratensians were the great colonizing Orders. With his eloquence, Bernard of Clairvaux had in the middle of the twelfth century made the Cistercians the western ideal of a monastic Order. Their way of life combined spiritual duties with hard agricultural labour, thereby opening to them a large field of activity in the remote forest regions. A firm organization permanently maintained the links between the mother house and the daughter monasteries. For this reason the Cistercian monasteries in Bohemia and Poland, founded mostly from western Germany, for many years remained alien elements ('Cistercians from Cologne'). But their dependence on the mother house enabled them to claim rights of exemption from the power of the temporal authority such as had not been customary hitherto, and this precedent paved the way for greater independence for the church in eastern Europe as a whole.

The rise of the upper clergy was also a result of the princes' need for trained diplomats. Sometimes they were selected individually by a ruler, but before long such appointments came to be linked institutionally with certain bishoprics, provostships or abbeys. The prelates of the church entered the local and imperial diets as chancellors or advisers of the princes. The decisive turning-point came in the early thirteenth century. Between 1210 and 1217 in Poland, in 1222 in Bohemia, and in 1231 in Hungary the rulers more or less recognized the special jurisdiction of the church, permitted the church to administer its property and, at least in Poland and Bohemia, allowed the bishops to be elected by the cathedral chapters. The bishops and abbots thus acquired political rights in church affairs equivalent to those of the lay nobility in secular matters. The clergy in eastern Europe had finally secured the prerequisites of independence and had become a separate estate largely free from lay control.

The confrontation with the monarchy gave the prelates feudal rights at the most favourable moment. This was the time when in eastern Europe the rise of the principalities and the development of territorial administration really got under way, using methods, forms of organization and legal institutions taken over from the twelfth-century German settlements on the lower Elbe. Hungary also was caught up in the movement, and throughout the East, archbishops, bishops and abbots profited from it. Although they failed to develop compact ecclesiastical territories into principalities like their German counterparts, they became wealthy landowners and with the help of their educated clerical staff often ran their estates more profitably than their secular neighbours did. An outstanding example among many is Bruno of Schauenburg, bishop of Olomouc, who colonized his Moravian diocese in the second half of the thirteenth century on feudal principles far in advance of what was customary elsewhere in eastern Europe at the time. The bishops of Wrocław (Breslau) also organized their territory of Neisse on similar lines at about the same period, and in the fourteenth century the same bishops bought principalities which not only added to their income but also improved their rank and status, as the archbishops of Gniezno had done earlier and the bishops of Cracow were later to do. Nor was this process confined to the episcopacy. By intensified exploitation of their lands and new acquisitions, the Premonstratensians, the Knights of St John, the Templars, the Teutonic Order, the Cistercians and the Benedictines also became rich landowners, and the church as a whole became a major economic force. It scarcely needs to be added that their activities contributed to the development of society as a whole in eastern and central Europe.

Together with the opening up of new territories went a strengthening of the parochial network, so that the ground under the feet of the leading churchmen became increasingly

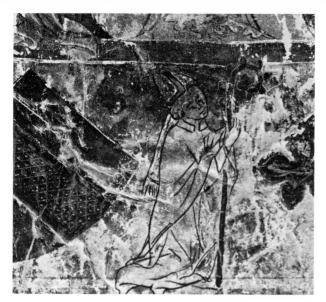

62 John Dražic, from his missal. After spending nine years in Avignon, the bishop returned to Prague with several French manuscripts which were highly influential in the development of Bohemian book illumination.

solid and their political influence substantial. Their position improved so much in the course of the thirteenth century that instead of merely attending the diets of the nobles they came to assume the first rank in the social hierarchy. Frequently it was the prelates who determined the fortunes of a country if the throne were vacant or royal policy was weak and vacillating.

Organized in this way on a territorial basis, the church identified itself with the fate of the national kingdoms which had sprung up on the ground left vacant by the declining Empire. Frequently the bishops were the champions of national unity, as for example in Poland in the thirteenth century. Organized on the same basis as the estates of the realm and playing a leading part in the social and political hierarchy of its country, the church developed a nationalistic note, even in its religion. The clergy soon developed a sharp ear for linguistic differences and defended its offices and livings against foreigners, generally against Germans in Poland and Bohemia and frequently also against Italians in Hungary. The archbishop of Gniezno, Jakób Świnka, and the bishop of Prague, John Dražic, were champions of a nationally orientated church policy at the beginning of the fourteenth century.

With the same object in mind the church encouraged the cult of saints of national importance: in Poland bishop Stanislav, in Bohemia duke Wenceslaus, in Hungary king Stephen. By providing national relics and places of pilgrimage (Często-chowa, Prague, Mariazell in Styria) the church offered each of the different peoples a special national cult within the all-embracing unity of cosmopolitan Catholicism. Simultaneously it encouraged each nation to prove itself the noblest member of the Catholic family by demonstrating its religious enthusiasm. As a result of their conflicts with the Mongols and the Turks and their own great expansion to the east and the south-east in the fourteenth century, the Hungarians and the Poles saw themselves as the frontier guards of Christianity; they were the *antemurale Christianitatis*, as the Hungarian chancery proudly announced about 1400. They were proud, moreover, to have remained uncontaminated by western heretical movements, though this in reality was an achievement due more to belated social development than to any special loyalty to the church.

In the region south of the Baltic, things proceeded differently. Here the development of church, state and civilization was strangely interwoven. In 1225 one of the local Polish princes,

63 The violent dismemberment of St Stanislav, one of Poland's most revered martyrs; woodcut from the *Vita Beatissimi Stanislai* (1511).

109

64 Rudolf IV of Habsburg;
this is probably
the first true portrait in
German painting (*c.* 1365).

Conrad of Masovia, had called upon the knights of the Teutonic
Order to help him against heathen Prussia and had rewarded
them with land. After prolonged and, in the end, very brutal
missionizing efforts, a highly organized state was developed
from these beginnings by the Teutonic knights, based in part at
least on the highly developed administration of Sicily. From the
early fourteenth century onwards the new Prussian state came
into conflict with the Polish kings in the region of the lower
Vistula and thereafter became a constant factor in Polish
politics. It took the Polish kings a hundred years of struggle to
drive the enemy back and another hundred years passed, after
their first successes in 1410 and 1422, before they succeeded in
incorporating the lands of the Teutonic Order into the Polish
state at the time of the Reformation. Until that date the peace
of Christendom in the Baltic region was repeatedly disturbed in
spite of papal mediation, and it is noteworthy that, in the
negotiations conducted under the pope's aegis at Warsaw in
1339 and at Constance in 1415, it was the Polish episcopacy
which argued their country's political claims against the
Teutonic knights.

In the second half of the fourteenth century central and
eastern Europe saw a generation of outstanding rulers. Casimir
the Great of Poland, Louis the Great of Hungary, Charles IV of

Bohemia are the most notable, but Rudolf IV of Habsburg in Austria, Winrich of Kniprode in Prussia, and Waldemar Atterdag in Denmark had similar plans and ambitions. All these rulers were deeply involved in power politics and the Hungarian, Polish and Bohemian kings initiated large-scale territorial expansion. But they also gave much attention to centralization of the administration and the promotion of a sense of national awareness and identity, for which preceding developments had prepared the way. They gathered the political fruits of the expansion of the economy and the growth of population which resulted from colonization, the founding of urban centres, and the influx of settlers from Germany, the Netherlands and Flanders. It was part of their policy to intensify national consciousness by visual means, by erecting splendid buildings, founding monasteries, rebuilding cathedrals (as was done by Charles IV in Prague, which became an archbishopric in 1344),

65, 66 The Old Town Bridge Tower (right) and the Parler choir of St Vitus cathedral (left) in Prague are among the outstanding architectural achievements of the cultural resurgence begun under Charles IV (1316–78).

but they also paid attention to cultural matters. This they did by summoning distinguished scholars to their courts and to the episcopal sees of their land, by establishing contacts with the eminent personalities of their age, but above all by founding universities (Prague 1348, Cracow 1364, Vienna 1365).

In the first place these ventures remained entirely within an ecclesiastical framework. Monastic and cathedral schools provided the foundations, the first colleges were endowed by cathedral chapters, and the teaching was supervised by the bishops. But culture in general and religious culture in particular was also coming to be regarded as a matter of national prestige. It was in this spirit that bishop John Dražic called Augustinian canons from Pavia to Raudnitz in Bohemia in 1333. They brought with them the Christian humanism of northern Italy, and Raudnitz quickly established itself as a centre from which new foundations were set up and existing foundations reformed throughout the whole of central Europe from Cracow to southern Germany. Religious literature in Czech was produced at Raudnitz, and it was with the collaboration of the canons of Raudnitz that the first Czech dictionary saw the light of day in the middle of the fourteenth century.

Another Order which helped to shape contemporary ideals of scholarship and soon entered into close relations with the universities, was the Carthusian. The Carthusian monastery of Mariengarten near Prague took charge of its Order's north German province which stretched as far as Reval. The courts of Casimir the Great and Louis the Great, but in particular that of Charles IV, encouraged these Orders in various ways and became centres at which early humanism was fostered.

An active Christian spirit of reflection and reform was present in this early humanism. It was seen in the person of the learned writer of hymns, John Jenstein, archbishop of Prague, who ended his days in a Roman monastery. Through their pastoral work the clergy brought the early humanism to a broad sector of the laity, among whom it took the form of an intensified mystical faith which was fostered by the Carthusians but which also left its mark upon the religious life of the old Orders. The Bohemian Cistercian abbey of Königsaal, for example, produced a devotional book which quickly came to be widely distributed, the *Malogranatum* (Pomegranate). It set out to show laymen the same way to perfection as was prescribed for monks by the rules of their Orders. The monastic way of life with its combination of work and prayer appealed particularly to the religious needs of large sections of the middle classes in the urbanized regions, in southern Poland, in northern Hungary and above all in Bohemia and Moravia, where, in the form of a new, 'bourgeois' piety, it quickly took shape as a protest against the wealth of the prelates and the aristocratic character of the church.

68 The Golden Bull of Charles IV (*c.* 1400) is one of the finest manuscripts produced in the court atelier of Wenceslaus IV in Prague. In the bottom margin of this manuscript page, the tiny figure of king Wenceslaus is enclosed in his initial and surrounded by his bath-maidens.

67 The new 'bourgeois' piety in Bohemia found its literary expression in such devotional books as the *Malogranatum*, ◄ written in 1402.

The character of particular reform movements has always been affected by the level of the social or ecclesiastical hierarchy from which they originated. Although all shared a common point of departure in the search for a new and better way of following Christ, it was in the nature of things that demands for reform were formulated differently depending on whether they were made by the pope, a bishop, an abbot or a country priest. To the layman the right road lay in yet another direction. In western Europe lay movements had been searching for 'the coming empire of peace' (B. Töpfer) ever since the year 1000, and sometimes their efforts had taken a radical form, turning with greater or lesser determination not only against the lay persecutors of the church but also against its over-worldly leaders. Such movements were usually led by monks and priests from the simple clergy; at any rate they did not have the support of many bishops.

The laity began to act with greater independence as it became aware of its role in society. This growth of awareness was connected with urban development and with the greater mobility available to the inhabitants of a town community. Since on the whole town life developed more slowly in the East, it is therefore not surprising that it took longer for a mobile, informed and receptive lay society to appear in eastern Europe than in the West. We first find it there in the fourteenth century and the most likely explanation of its appearance is the process of adjustment between East and West which followed the great changes in agrarian society during the two preceding centuries.

In the West the laity was helped to solve the social problems of town life by the activities of the two great mendicant Orders, the Franciscans and the Dominicans. These Orders differed radically from conventional monasticism, particularly in the early decades of their development, and spread with unexpected rapidity in eastern and central Europe. The first

Dominican friary north of the Alps was set up in 1217; by 1219 the Order had become established in Hungary and by 1227 there was a Polish Dominican province. In Germany the two German successors of St Dominic introduced the Order in the regions both west and east of the Elbe. The Franciscans also spread rapidly. In the 1230s there were already enough settlements in Bohemia and Poland for the Order to establish a joint province. Almost simultaneously two princesses joined the new Order, encouraged charitable work and were canonized after their death (Agnes of Bohemia, d. 1270; Margaret of Hungary, d. 1282). But this very fact shows how the mendicant Orders in eastern Europe had changed their original character. Caring for the sick and poor and occasional missionary work (for example, in Lithuania) were worthy causes; but social welfare was very different from the social protest for the sake of which they had at first pursued the ideal of poverty.

The Waldensian lay preachers, on the other hand, continued to pursue the original ideal. But the Waldensian movement, although it began in the West about 1172, did not reach eastern Europe until the fourteenth century. And the Flagellants, although found in the East as early as the end of the thirteenth century, not long after their first appearance in Italy about 1260, did not forsake the paths of orthodoxy until the middle of the fourteenth century, here or elsewhere.

But in the long run the rationalism of scholastic theology was of little help to untrained minds in their search for religious involvement, and the tendency was therefore to concentrate on mystical introspection. In doing so it was all too easy to transcend the dividing line between orthodoxy and pantheistic heresy. Even notable theologians of the age like Meister Eckhart or Jan van Ruysbroek did not escape this danger; how much more was this true of simpler minds! Some, like the 'Brethren of the Free Spirit', strayed into libertine ways, and though this was exceptional, many others were suspect to the ecclesiastical authorities, particularly the Beguine movement. The Beguines were pious female penitents who led a life that was frequently hard, in monastic conditions but without ecclesiastical control and often even without firm rules. They were prevalent, and evidently popular. In 1332 the Inquisition investigating the Silesian Beguines uncovered a far-flung network of settlements stretching right across the heart of Europe from Prague to Cologne. In Hungary, too, the Beguine movement was widespread, and among the Beghards (the male lay mendicant movement) there is evidence of similar links.

This was one form of lay devotion, the orthodoxy of which was difficult to test. At another level the demand of the laity for an independent religious life of their own produced devotional literature. Vernacular literature in Poland and Hungary in the fourteenth century began with translations of the Bible and the copying of sermons. Bohemia was even more advanced in this respect, and several translations of the Bible into German and Czech have survived, as well as prayers and hymns. Particularly significant are the works of the Czech nobleman, Thomas of Štítný (d. 1401). Here the individual's relations with God are

69 A father teaches his three sons; manuscript page from Thomas of Štítný's theological and philosophical reflections. His writings mark the establishment of a Czech vernacular.

70 'The Harvest of Death' is the central theme of *The Ploughman of Bohemia*, an important work of early humanist German literature (*c.* 1460). Under the impact of his young wife's death, the author, Johannes of Saaz, engages in a dialogue with God, complaining about the injustice of death, and succeeds in transferring a purely personal experience on to a general human level.

taken out of the purely ecclesiastical sphere and transferred to the everyday life of the ordinary citizen. The same emancipation of religious thought from the intermediacy of the church and the same direct confrontation between the faithful and God, is seen in the famous *Gespräch des Ackermanns mit dem Tod* (Ackermann's Conversation with Death), written in Bohemia in this period, which is the most important work of early modern High German literature. Bohemian town civilization, the high level of which can be judged from the fact that there were thirty-seven urban schools of Latin in the country at the beginning of the fifteenth century, produced a literature which could hold its own by the most exacting western standards.

By far the most important centre was Prague; it was the most populous city east of the Rhine, the residence of the emperor, a university town, and a nodal-point at the intersection of some of the most important European trade routes. Charles IV personally summoned the well-known Augustinian canon Konrad Waldhauser (d. 1369) to Prague from Austria as a reform preacher. Through his activities at a school for preachers Konrad influenced the whole country and found a successor of at least equal stature in canon Milič Kremsier. With the help of pious donations to which the emperor himself contributed, Milič acquired a whole district in the city of Prague, and there he collected together the poor and outcast in a 'new Jerusalem'. Perhaps it was here that the Dutch mystic Gert Groote or some of his close collaborators became acquainted with the mixture of work, poverty and pious instruction which later spread to the north-west and became famous as the Dutch *devotio moderna*.

The clergy resisted the new moral rigorism. Even Konrad Waldhauser was called to Rome to explain his activities and Milič died on his third visit to the pope to defend himself (1374). His community was dissolved, but the preachers' movement lived on under Matthias of Janov (d. 1394), finding followers among students, young ecclesiastics and bourgeois

71 In the Gradual of Malá Strana (1572), a song in honour of Jan Hus, the Czech reformer is represented between Wycliffe and Luther, an indication of the link between the European protest movements.

72 The Týn church in Prague, founded in the second half of the fourteenth century by the German citizens of the Old Town, became the main Hussite church during the uprising.

benefactors. In 1391 in Prague they endowed a preaching centre especially for Czech vernacular, 'The Innocent Children', the Bethlehem chapel. The hall held 3,000 people. In 1402 the young university teacher Jan Hus was installed here as preacher.

Hus combined learned discussion of reform at the university, which at that time still had an international student body, with pastoral work for the laity. He was particularly impressed by reading Wycliffe (d. 1384), although he confined himself mainly to the English theologian's moral criticism. The Bohemian queen, by birth a Bavarian princess, was among his audience and the archbishop made him preacher of the Synod. Although Hus was not, to begin with, 'leader' of the movement later named after him but only one of a critical generation of mostly Czech university teachers, he was caught in 1408 in the mills of church disciplinary proceedings; in 1409 he was excommunicated and in 1410 banished. In 1412, like Luther after him, he attacked the sale of indulgences and thereby lost

119

the favour of the Bohemian king who shared in the practice. In 1412 he appealed to Christ against the pope's decision, not as a desperate gesture, but to affirm a principle which had already been evoked in 1409 by a German theologian against the Council of Pisa. Like his connection with Wycliffe, this action shows how the Bohemian reform movement was part of a wider movement running through the length and breadth of Europe.

Meanwhile in 1409 a dispute over livings and votes at the university which concerned professors rather than students had led the three non-Bohemian *nationes* (or student associations) to leave Prague by way of protest. After losing about half its members the university was influenced more strongly than before by the 'Wycliffites', but it was only in 1413 that the orthodox Czech theology professors lost control. By then Hus had already become a symbol. Because of him Prague was in danger of being placed under an interdict. He was forced to live in the country under noble protection, the possibility of a civil war could not be ruled out, and in the autumn of 1414, in an almost hopeless situation, he appealed to the general Council of Constance.

In 1412 and 1413, following the treatise of Wycliffe, Hus had collected his views on the church (*De Ecclesia*) and in the process had raised afresh a basic issue of Christian theology which had preoccupied ecclesiastics ever since Augustine – the issue of the institutional church versus the spiritual community of good men. As early as the eleventh century Berengar of Tours had argued that a mortal sinner cannot legitimately exercise church functions. This contention, which could have destroyed the entire organization of the priesthood, had been presented ever since as a particularly dangerous heresy. Whether Hus himself intended to draw such a conclusion, is not clear. But even so his views, which he derived from Wycliffe, amounted to an attack on the hierarchically organized church and its claim to mediate between God and man. Hus therefore went to Constance to face a serious charge.

In Constance he was imprisoned illegally. Instead of being allowed to have the discussion he had demanded, he was simply interrogated. In spite of all his judges' efforts he refused to recant and thereby to expose the entire Bohemian reform movement to a verdict of heresy; and in the conscious knowledge of inward superiority he went to his death at the stake (6 July 1415).

The Bohemian reform movement proceeded undaunted. Master Jakoubek ze Stříbra (Jacobellus of Mies) became Hus's successor in Prague; the power of the Bohemian barons protected the reformers. Communion in both kinds – the chalice as well as the wafer for the laity – became their symbol and also, because it brought with it excommunication by the old church, the criterion of their determination. By 1419 the religious communities had been formed in many places all over the country, usually without opposition. Prague university, which all the opponents of reform had meanwhile left, became (in Bartoš' phrase) their 'controlling authority'. Half-hearted measures of restraint on the part of the Bohemian king who had so far remained more or less passive resulted in open opposition from the reformers. In the months that followed, the whole country was thrown into chaos.

Worn out with anxiety Wenceslaus IV died in 1419. For the next seventeen years Bohemia existed as a '*de facto* republic' (R. Urbánek) in opposition to the legitimate claimant to the throne, Wenceslaus' brother, the emperor Sigismund. This alone was an unheard-of rebellion against the whole monarchical system of government and a sign of the political strength of the revolution. In wars fought by both sides with the utmost cruelty the 'Hussites', in possession of most of Bohemia, withstood five western crusades. In spite of internal differences, foreign pressure welded them together, occasionally even leading to an alliance with the country's Catholic party (1421). Finally, in 1426 the revolution went over to the offensive, threatening the whole of central Europe with military expeditions in all directions. Because it received support from the lower ranks of the rural and urban population and in Silesia even from the princes, it seemed all the more dangerous to the constituted powers.

When discussions with the Hussites finally began in 1432, they were undertaken by a new reform Council at Basel which did not represent conservative Europe so much as the democratic reforming elements in the church, particularly the lower clergy and the universities. For this reason the peace concluded between the Hussites and the Council was not ratified by the pope.

What made peace possible was the existence of internal differences among the Hussites. On the one side there was a 'moderate' group (variously known as 'Utraquists' or 'Calixtines') under the influence of Jacobellus of Mies, which was particularly strong at the university and in the old city of Prague. Although difficult to define socially, its character was determined by the upper classes, and it pursued reform only to the extent that was necessary. Its most important dogmatic characteristic was the subordination of the pope's authority and Catholic tradition to the Scriptures. It recognized the opportunist archbishop of Prague as its legitimate head so as to preserve the apostolic succession of its priests; but when Jan Rokycana (d. 1471) was elected by the diet in 1435 as his successor, he was not recognized by the pope.

If the moderates were strong in Prague, the radicals were strong in the countryside, where they were grouped around mountains with Biblical names (Tabor, Horeb, Mons Olivetti), and later around the newly founded city of Tabor. As Kalivoda has emphasized, their programme of freedom and equality already contained the germs of future revolutionary democracy. By electing a bishop they broke the ecclesiastical succession. Later they organized themselves in city confederations, maintained standing armies under important leaders (Jan Žižka, d. 1424; Procop the Great, d. 1434), and quickly brought order into the chiliastic activism of the early period. In place of the Catholic doctrine of the real presence of Christ in the Eucharist they substituted his effective presence; they rejected penance, the last sacrament, purgatory and intercessory prayers. But in 1434 they were defeated by the Bohemian Catholics and 'moderates', and it was this defeat which made possible the compromise with the Council of Basel.

The compromise of 1436, known as 'the Compacts of Basel', was based on the Four Articles of Prague of 1420, the joint programme of the 'moderates' and the 'radicals'. These four articles – which constituted (as may be said) a milestone in the 'democratization' of Europe – can be formulated as (1) freedom for the chalice, (2) freedom for the sermon, (3) liberation from the temporal power of the church and (4) equality for all before the law. In spite of all compromises, their recognition at Basel opened the age of confessionalism in Europe.

A small community with the lay hermit Peter Chelčický at its head remained outside the Compacts and also outside the Prague Articles. But it was not until 1457 that the group was firmly organized as the 'Community of Bohemian Brethren'. By doing simple manual work and living together, the brethren followed the example of earlier lay movements; more radical in their theology than other groups, they were close to the future Calvinists. It was not until 1575 that they were expressly tolerated in Bohemia, even by the Hussites.

But it was not its theology so much as its constitutional policy that made the Hussite movement revolutionary. For the first time in European history subjects justified resistance to legitimate authority on grounds of faith; and this religious justification gave revolutionary force to the traditional right of resistance claimed by the estates. Here the Hussites were claiming a right which was again used to legitimize resistance during the Reformation, by the French Huguenots, in the Netherlands, and in the English revolution.

For a generation the Hussite revolution seems to have made a deep impression on public opinion in Europe. Hussite doctrines had a certain following in Moravia, Silesia and Slovakia; later they were introduced into Hungary and Rumania by

Hussite mercenaries. There were more Wycliffites and Hussites at Cracow university than at any other university, but it was not long before they were attacked by the Polish church, the Polish king and the Polish nobility. The cities of Poland showed little interest in Hussitism, just as later they remained passive in the Lutheran Reformation. Such criticism of the church and society as occurred in Poland at a later date stemmed from the artists and scholars of the Italian Renaissance.

In the West there were many isolated links between English and Bohemian Wycliffites (Lord Oldcastle, executed 1410; Pavel Kravář, burnt at St Andrews 1433; Peter Payne, Oxford Master, who in 1413 fled to Bohemia where he died in 1457). In Belgium, whence 'free-thinkers' (Picardists) had come to Bohemia in 1418, the Inquisition also took action against Hussite propaganda in the 1420s. Paradoxically Joan of Arc threatened the Hussites with a crusade not long before she herself died at the stake. Her militant nationalism had something in common with that of the 'right wing' of the Hussites whose views were expounded with great rhetorical skill in the manifestoes of the old city of Prague between 1419 and 1421.

But in spite of this nationalism, the religious and social approach of the Hussite revolution was nowhere as popular as in Germany. A number of the leading Taborite theologians were Germans. Some two dozen German Hussite priests are known to us by name, and in the middle of the fifteenth century, probably in collaboration with German Waldensians, they organized their followers under three secret bishops. Even after the failure in 1471 of the 'Hussite king', George of Poděbrad, to save Hussitism as a political force and to enlist for it the sympathies of the German princes, the link between the Bohemian heretics and Germany lived on among simple people as well as among scholars. When Luther proposed 'truly to take charge of the Bohemians' cause' so as to 'join them to us and us to them' he was only emphasizing the historical connection between the Bohemian heresy and the world-shaking movement of the Reformation.

# IV ECONOMIC RELATIONS BETWEEN EASTERN AND WESTERN EUROPE

*M. M. Postan*

The history of the economic relations of western and eastern Europe cannot be told as a simple or even a continuous story. These relations did not develop similarly and did not play the same role in the economic life of different parts of Europe and at different points of time in the Middle Ages. In general, trade between west European and east European territories affected economic life and social conditions more powerfully after the eleventh century than before. Furthermore, the economic effects went deeper in the north and centre of Europe than in its southern regions.

The chronological difference is something most historians would take for granted. It is generally assumed that trade – all trade – grew in volume and importance from century to century, and was therefore more abundant and had greater economic effect in the later Middle Ages than in the so-called Dark Ages. What is perhaps not so generally accepted is that the more southerly currents of east–west trade should have played a relatively subordinate part in the economic development of the continent as a whole and of its main regions taken separately. It is an accepted tradition of economic historiography to focus attention on the story of the Mediterranean or Levantine trade and to treat its development as the main theme of European commercial history. This preferential treatment of southern trade by historians is easily explained. It abounds with episodes familiar to the readers and writers of popular history, and touches upon some of the best known political and cultural landmarks in the Middle Ages, such as the rise and progress of the Italian commercial cities, their role in the crusades, the spread of Near Eastern manners, tastes and learning. The record

73 St Adalbert presents a Jewish slave trader to Boleslav I Chrobry; from a relief on the twelfth-century bronze doors of Gniezno cathedral.

of this trade is also strongly tinted with the romance which clings to all evidence of traffic with the Orient. For it was by the southern routes that men of western Europe were able to come into personal, indeed physical, contact with the Moslem East, North Africa and central Asia, and more indirectly with India and China.

Yet the purely economic and social importance of this trade was not so great as its romantic and picturesque appeal. The flow of commodities brought in or taken out by the southern trade currents washed over Europe without irrigating the main fields of economic activity outside the Mediterranean world itself, and without greatly accelerating the motion of social change. Except for bullion, few of the incoming goods were in the nature of essential commodities catering for the necessities of life. They were mostly spices, exotic fruits, silks, brocades, and a few other costly artifacts of oriental workmanship, and they served the demand for luxuries of the rich and the power-ful: princes, ecclesiastical institutions and dignitaries and feudal chieftains. To this extent the southern trade was, so to speak, outside the mainstream of economic activity serving the needs of the medieval population *en masse* and the medieval economy as a whole. Indeed some imports need not have served any western needs at all but were merely goods in transit. The most valuable of these (for a long time they were probably the most valuable of all imports) were the east European slaves. The slave traffic as a rule originated in and traversed other parts of Europe on its way to the countries of the Moslem Levant.

The exports of western Europe to pay for the eastern imports were as a rule equally peripheral to its economy and its society. In some periods, more especially in the earlier centuries of the Middle Ages, the balance of trade was probably in favour of the East and therefore set up an outflow of currency and precious metals. Gold and silver apart, western Europe, especially in the earlier centuries, had little to sell to the East: some weapons, some horses, a little food, later some cloth and linen. In the aggregate, these exports were neither large nor very valuable and their procurement did not call for an outlay of labour or other resources on a scale large enough to exert a pressure on economic social processes in Europe, whether western or eastern.

74 Medieval trade routes.

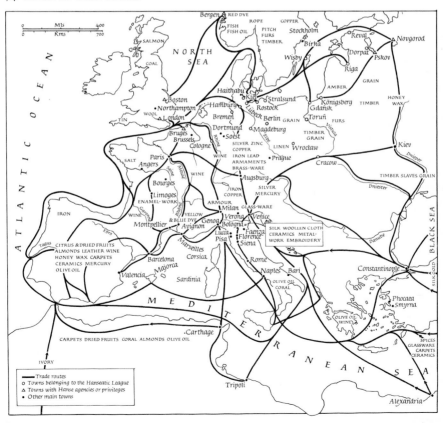

However, from this point of view – that of economic and social processes – a distinction must be drawn between the two variants of the southern trade current. One of the currents was sea-borne, for it led from southern French, Catalan and above all Italian seaports across the Mediterranean to the Levant or North Africa; the other was mainly earth-bound and led from western Europe to the East across the land-mass of south-eastern Europe. Of the two variants, the maritime may have carried goods of greater worth and contributed to the development of the Italian city-states, a more conspicuous monument to its achievements than the goods and urban civilizations involved in the land route. But it was, geographically speaking, a one-step movement, a single link directly connecting the Mediterranean with Byzantium and the Moslem East. It did not, therefore, draw to its traffic, or otherwise touch upon, any country or region of eastern Europe. On the other hand the land-borne route to and from the Orient went over the various territories of south-eastern Europe – mostly Slavic – and deposited in them some commodities and took from them some of their produce. For that reason alone, the various parts of continental Europe felt its impact and were bound to be influenced by it.

The countries thus drawn into the oriental trade of Europe were Bohemia, Hungary, South Poland (Malopolska), and, in the end, southern Russia. The order in which these regions have been arranged here is of course that of their relative positions in the west–east direction; but this purely geographical order also happens to coincide with the chronology of their economic development and the timing of their links with the trans-continental trade.

In this order, Bohemia and Moravia were the first regions to be drawn into the traffic. Indeed so early was Bohemia's economic development, compared with that of the more easterly regions, and so much of its development was influenced by German merchants and rulers, that from some points of view Bohemia, and in fact the whole of the area along the

Sudeten and Carpathian belt, could with justice be considered as belonging to the western end of the east–west connection. In fact its trade connections and the network of its principal routes ran in every direction, not only to the east but also south to the Mediterranean via Vienna and Venice, to the north mainly by the Elbe, and to the west mainly to the Bavarian towns of Augsburg, Nuremberg and Rothenburg.

Bohemia's contacts with the world outside, to the west as well as to the east, were bound to quicken with the opening of her silver mines in the thirteenth century, when Jihtnovo and Kutna Hora grew to become very important sources of newly mined bullion. The range over which Bohemia's silver circulated, and the imports for which it paid, can only be guessed and not precisely allocated. It is, however, a fair guess that until the turn of the fourteenth and fifteenth centuries, when the silver mines rapidly gave out, the supplies of bullion and the excellent silver currency based on it must have stimulated the long-distance exchanges with both East and West. It would, of course, be an exaggeration to ascribe the commercial development of the Bohemian economy in the thirteenth and fourteenth centuries, and the growth of towns – Prague, Brno and Bratislava – wholly to the long-distance trade and more particularly to the trade along the southern routes to and from the Orient. But it must have been Prague's position along that route that drew to it, from the very earliest Middle Ages, merchants from both the Moslem East and the West. It also provided an additional attraction to German urban settlers and merchants who flocked to Bohemian cities throughout the Middle Ages.

The regions immediately to the east and north-east of Bohemia – Silesia, Hungary, South Poland, and southernmost Russia – played a part in the east-bound traffic which differed from that played by Bohemia only in its timing and scale. Silesia developed somewhat later than Bohemia: the high-water mark of its economic expansion was in the fourteenth century. But that expansion also depended to some extent on    129 the output of Silesian mines and on Silesia's position at the intersection of several important trade routes. Some of the latter led to the north-east into northern Poland and from there to western Russia, more particularly to the region of Volhynia; other routes led north and north-west into the German regions along the west Baltic Sea. Some of the routes, however, tapped and supplied the regions in the south-west. Above all Wrocław (Breslau) gathered to itself much of the trade from Bohemia, Hungary and South Poland, and indirectly also to and from Russia and the transpontine outposts of Byzantium. These channels carried eastern goods which were frequently re-exported further west or north-west by local and Prussian merchants.

Next along the west–east route lay Hungary. Hungary's development, like that of other parts of eastern Europe, was predominantly agricultural, and its trade with other regions was largely based on the agricultural produce of its prairies, mainly grain, cattle and horses. But Hungarian trade also benefited from the opening up of the Transylvanian deposits of silver and copper, and from its geographical position on the way to the Danube valley and the shores of the Black Sea.

The geographical position on the approaches to southern Russia and the Black Sea also favoured the east-borne trade of southern Poland. Cracow, for long Poland's most important urban centre, rose to commercial eminence very early in the Middle Ages, possibly before the end of the first millennium. It appears to have harboured colonies of foreign merchants of oriental origin, Armenians, Jews and Greeks, in the very earliest periods of its history. We must assume that what drew these motley foreigners into Cracow was the facilities it provided for the importation and re-exportation of goods from other countries. Cracow's facilities for trade to the east eventually came to be shared and even excelled by the town of Lwow, a more easterly rival of Cracow which was greatly fostered by the Polish kings of the thirteenth century and eventually became

the most important entrepôt centre for trade to the plains of

75 Cloisonné enamel pendant made in Kiev (eleventh or twelfth century).

southern Russia and Moldavia. In general, South Poland served in the later Middle Ages as the principal approach to southern Russia and, above all, to the commercial centres at the estuaries of the Danube, Dnieper and Don. Eventually it was through these estuary towns and by way of the Polish termini that most of the eastern goods destined for the West were carried. The Polish involvement with the economic fortunes of south-west Russia became closer still with the conquest of a great part of this region by Casimir the Great in 1347.

The high-water mark of south Russian trade, or at any rate of the trade centred in the interior of southern Russia, was somewhat earlier, in the period between the tenth and early thirteenth centuries, when Kiev and the Kievan principality were at the height of their political power and economic development. From the very early centuries of Varangian rule in southern Russia, i.e. from the middle of the ninth century, Kievan Russia appeared to draw to itself large quantities of oriental luxuries: how large they were is shown by numerous archaeological finds of recent years. Literary sources also testify to the presence in Kiev at the earliest times of merchants from distant lands. It may well be, of course, that Kiev was not the sole point of attraction for oriental goods or oriental merchants. According to a Russian chronicle, a ninth-century prince, Sviatoslav, extolled the attractions of Perejaslavl on the Dnieper in preference to Kiev as an emporium for eastern luxuries. Historians, however, have every reason for considering Kiev at the height

131

of its prosperity, i.e. in the twelfth century, as the principal terminus of the southern trade route by which eastern goods travelled to the West.

Kiev and Kievan Russia lost this role in the course of the late thirteenth and fourteenth centuries. For this, some blame must be attached to the political disorders brought about by the rivalries and wars between the south Russian principalities. The transfer of the political and economic centre of gravity of Russia to the north-east, to the regions of Vladimir and Suzdal, also contributed to the demise of Kiev. But it was the conquest of south Russia by the Tatars in the mid-thirteenth century that dealt the heaviest blow to the economic prosperity and commercial role of Kievan Russia.

The decline of Kiev as a terminus of the southern route did not, however, bring about any noticeable decline in the trade flowing along it. It merely enhanced the relative importance of the alternative channels. Of the latter, the one which traversed the north of Europe and tapped the eastern supplies through the Volga and in north-western Russia, will be dealt with later, in the context of northern trade. The other channel, however, was well to the south of Kiev, by the northern littoral of the Black Sea and the estuaries of the rivers flowing into it. On the estuary of the Dnieper there was the Byzantine outpost of Cherson (the Russian Korsun), on the estuary of the Don there was Tmutarakan, and on the Volga there was the Venetian factory of Tana.

More important than any of these was the Genoese port of Caffa on the Crimean coast with its satellites at the estuaries of the Danube and the Dniester in Moldavia. In the course of time the Genoese, harboured and protected as they were by the rulers of the Tatar Horde, and favoured by their powerful position in Byzantium and the Mediterranean, succeeded in building up Caffa as one of the largest, though also one of the least famed of medieval commercial centres. At the apogee of its development in the fourteenth century, its population may well have exceeded thirty thousand. Its exports comprised the entire gamut of south Russian products. Grain was apparently shipped to the eastern Mediterranean and occasionally to Italy; forest and other products of the Russian interior, such as furs and wax, also found their way there. But it was slaves who provided the mainstay of the trade and the bulk of its profits.

The importance of the trade and its volume can be judged from the fact that, according to literary sources at Cordoba in Spain, which was only one of many recipients of the human cargoes from Russia, the numbers of slaves at one time in the ninth century exceeded 14,000. And although the slave trade may have declined in the course of the late fourteenth and fifteenth centuries, a Portuguese traveller who visited Caffa in the fifteenth century, Pero Tafur, could still describe with great wonder the abundant volume of the slave traffic from the south Russian plains to Caffa and from there to the various countries of the Near and Middle East.

By that time, however, Caffa had already declined, and much of its erstwhile trade shifted to its Moldavian outposts of Akerman, Tighina and Kilia. In 1475 the Turkish conquest of the entire Pontine region, following the earlier Russian conquest and sack of the Venetian factory of Tana, wound up both the Italian termini of the southern route. But in the two or three centuries preceding the violent collapse of the Italian presence, that presence not only fed the transcontinental route across southern Europe with goods of oriental origin but also linked that route with its maritime alternative across the Mediterranean, and helped to create a single system of routes and exchanges binding the sources of oriental luxuries with their western markets.

To speak of this route as I have done here, region by region, each figuring mainly as a stage in the transcontinental progress of oriental goods, must distort the true story of economic development. To repeat what I have already pointed out, the bulk of the traffic circulating along the roads and rivers must to an overwhelming extent have been made up of goods which were, so to speak, indigenous, i.e. products of local agriculture, forestry and mining. Most of these goods served local markets within the regions themselves. Some of the local goods may have overflowed into long-distance channels, but the overflow was not great or powerful enough to influence the shape of indigenous economies and societies in any substantial way. If we consider the history of east-bound trade from the point of view of the impact it made upon economic development, the trade currents which circulated across northern Europe were of greater importance. They were closely bound up with the general eastward expansion of western European states, with the migration of population, with the opening up of the continental interior of central and eastern Europe, and with the inauguration of large-scale exchanges of essential and bulky commodities. A trade thus rooted in general economic development was bound not only to affect the economic fortunes of the regions it traversed but also to be affected by them.

THE NORTHERN ROUTE: ECONOMIC GEOGRAPHY

The history of economic relations between eastern and western Europe across its northern and central regions is part of a more general movement of historical change. It reflects almost every aspect of medieval development: its geography, its economic processes, its political transformations, its institutional framework, its social system. Indeed, so wide was the spectrum of economic influences radiating from the north-west to the north-east, that any attempt to single out the history of trade may appear to simplify the situation to the point of distortion.

Most conspicuous of all were the changes in the geographical pattern of the east-borne trade of northern and central Europe, or rather in the territorial boundaries within which it operated and spread and in the routes along which it flowed. The frontiers marking off the trading areas, and the routes linking them, were not wholly identical with political boundaries and were not always created by military conquest and political occupation. Yet there is little doubt that as the principalities of north-western Europe extended their military and political power to central and eastern Europe, the territorial range of medieval commerce expanded accordingly.

From this geo-political standpoint, the history of north European trade falls into three clearly discernible stages. The initial stage coincides with the Dark Ages proper – the four or five centuries which followed the irruption and settlement of Germanic tribes in western Europe. During that period inter-regional trade was in all probability very meagre, and such little long-distance trade as northern and western Europe knew circulated almost wholly within the limits of the former Roman empire.

In general, documentary or archaeological evidence of the interregional commerce of northern Europe in the Dark Ages is sparse. We are told a little about the commercial activities of the Frisian inhabitants of the Rhine estuary, who provided some economic links between northern Europe (England, the Low Countries and possibly Scandinavia) on the one hand, and southern Germany and perhaps northern Italy on the other. We are also told about Anglo-Saxon merchants trading with the regions across the narrow seas, and Scandinavian seafarers trading with England and Ireland. But of direct commercial contacts between north-west Europe and lands further east we have hardly any evidence at all. Within eastern Europe the Scandinavians traded over long distances, though until the era of the Viking raids in the ninth and tenth centuries, their long-distance expeditions and trade were directed mainly south-eastwards to the markets of Byzantium and indirectly to those of the Moslem Levant. The subjugation of Russia by the Swedish Varangians in the ninth century may or may not have been a wholly commercial venture, but it was undoubtedly bound up with Scandinavian trading voyages. In the subsequent two centuries the Scandinavians travelled and traded along the river routes across the plains of Russia, and in this way

76 Irish or Northumbrian bronze bucket (c. 800), found in a grave in the Scandinavian town of Birka; one of several finds indicating economic contact between Anglo-Saxon countries and Scandinavia.

established commercial links with Constantinople and possibly also with other Byzantine regions in the Balkans, and with the Hellenistic succession states between the Volga and the Caspian.

How great this eastward trade was is indirectly suggested by the vast hoards of coinage, mostly Arab, found buried in Scandinavian, mostly Swedish, sites and along the routes to the east frequented by the Scandinavians. In the area of Scandinavian domicile some 1,700 hoards, containing on an average some 300 mostly eastern coins, have so far been found, and we must assume that the coins so hoarded formed only a proportion of the bullion and coinage the Scandinavians acquired in the course of their trade and voyages.

This trade was not focused in urban centres housing professional merchants to the same extent as it was to be in feudal Europe two or three centuries later. Some trading ports did, however, emerge on the Scandinavian trade routes. Whether they were real urban settlements, or merely haphazard huddles of wattle cabins, we do not know. Nor can we be certain that

77 Eleventh-century
Byzantine silver reliquary
from Gästrikland.

78 Hoard of Arabic coins found in Gotland (eighth and ninth centuries).

79 Ninth-century glass beakers and pottery imported from the mouth of the Rhine, found in Birka, a prominent Viking trading centre.

80 Hulk, cog and Viking warship on coins found in Haithabu.

they were regularly visited by Scandinavians; some may have been no more than local trading stations frequented by local fishermen and sailors. But the town of Wisby on the Isle of Gotland was obviously a commercial centre, and is specifically described as a trading settlement in the Life of St Anskarius. So may also have been places such as Dortic, Haithabu, Birka on Lake Malar, the port of Volyn ('*in finibus Slavorum*'), Truso, visited at the end of the ninth century by an emissary of the king of Wessex, or Reric, possibly situated in the vicinity of the later city of Lübeck.

Some of these 'towns' were situated in Slavic lands, but how far the native population of principalities ruled by the Scandinavians, particularly the principality of Kiev, actively participated in transcontinental trade, is difficult to tell. Between the tenth and the end of the twelfth century, as we have seen, Kiev had become an important trade centre. But there is very little evidence that other Slav principalities directly imported western merchandise or exported their own products to the West before the eleventh century; and there is little evidence of Kiev merchants engaging in long-distance trade. The only indigenous societies of eastern Europe to which early medieval documentary sources (mostly Arabic and Byzantine) impute a commerical role, were the Bulgars of the middle Volga and the Hazars of the lower Volga – the latter Jewish by religion and harbouring colonies of Jewish merchants.

138

Yet even the Hazar trade to the West was not considerable enough in quantity to leave a clear impression in the surviving evidence. Oriental goods from Byzantium and trans-Caspian Asia probably came in that way, but the export of slaves is virtually the only well-documented trade originating in the Volga regions. These regions probably formed the principal base from which, between the eighth and the eleventh centuries, but mainly in the tenth, the Jewish merchants (the Rhadanites) operated. According to Arab Jewish sources of the period, the Rhadanites drove their caravans of slaves westwards across the entire continent of Europe to destinations as remote as Moslem Spain, or eastwards to central Asia and China.

We must therefore assume that, for all the romance clinging to trade routes and trading societies so remote in place and time, the commercial exchanges they supported were not and could not have been of very great importance to either western or eastern Europe and did very little to make them economically interdependent. Apart from slaves destined for Moslem markets, the eastern exports by this route or similar exports by the southern route were probably confined to a few luxury goods of Byzantine and Near Eastern provenance. For its part, western Europe apparently sent very little of its own produce to the

81 Ninth-century armlets from a silver hoard in Gotland. The spiral ones were imported from eastern Europe.

East. From the tenth century onwards, gold and silver, mostly coined, apparently formed north-western Europe's *quid pro quo* for such goods as reached it from or via eastern Europe. This, at any rate, is the conclusion to be drawn from the evidence provided by the vast gold hoards of this period, which have been found in Scandinavia and Scandinavian-dominated countries of eastern Europe. The evidence of the hoards also suggests that at some period before the middle of the eleventh century the Scandinavian trade changed its direction or its centre of gravity. For whereas in the earlier hoards (and we have seen how vast they were) coins of eastern provenance, mostly Arabic, predominated, the later hoards contain mainly western, largely English coinage. It is probable, however, that much of the bullion in the later hoards came from booty or the proceeds of tributes, such as the English geld levied by Scandinavian conquerors. If so, the changed composition of the hoards may merely reflect the effect of the Norsemen's military and political activities in the West. We know, however, that in the eleventh century the supply of Arab coins dried up elsewhere as well, as a result of economic crises and political difficulties in the Arab empire.

Nevertheless, the very quantity of the hoarded gold and silver, whatever its origin, goes to demonstrate how one-sided the Scandinavian traffic must have been. Confined to rare and costly 'non-essential' commodities, it did not – indeed could not – do much to form or to transform the shape of Europe's economies or the structure of its societies. It is therefore not surprising that our records should be silent about merchants from the north-west voyaging to the Slav countries and beyond. Considered as networks of commercial connections, or what Germans call *Verkehrsgebiete*, the two areas – the western and the eastern – were to all intents and purposes self-contained spheres of commercial intercourse, brought into loose and intermittent contact by trade in slaves, luxuries and bullion.

Closer links between the two spheres, their eventual merger into a single commercial region, and the corresponding transformation of their internal economies and societies, were not to come until the next phase, roughly corresponding to what historians call the High Middle Ages, i.e. the period between the end of the tenth and the end of the thirteenth centuries. This was a period of manifold growth, favoured by several convergent factors. Relative stability came to Europe in the tenth century after 150–200 years of political disruption and of Moslem, Magyar and Norse invasions and conquests. The feudal order which emerged by the eleventh century at the end of a turbulent period of anarchy, offered sufficient peace and stability to make it possible for populations to grow, for settlement and reclamation of marginal land to proceed, and for trade, both local and interregional, to revive.

Before long, the states and societies of north-western Europe began to expand beyond their eastern borders. The *Drang nach Osten* was at first political in motive. The political and military frontiers of western Europe were being continually pushed out to the east until they reached the fringes of what in modern times has come to be considered as Polish and Russian territory. But the military and political conquest merely anticipated and facilitated other movements of expansion. Of these movements, that of colonization was probably the most far-reaching and enduring. But in the wake of conquering armies and colonizing peasants came also the culture of north-western Europe, mainly derived from western Christianity and Latin or German speech and writing; and with the sword and the Holy Writ and the peasant's plough came the merchandise.

In this story of territorial expansion, the episodes best known to students of history (best known because they have been well told by chroniclers and are clearly reflected in the political map of Europe) were the military ones. The military conquests and political acquisitions in the east began while the Carolingian empire was still in its prime and while its objectives still lay within the Germanic homeland, mainly in the territories of the Saxon tribes, between the Weser and the Elbe. By the end of the tenth century or perhaps even a little earlier, the Saxon

82 German eastward expansion.

lands had been fully absorbed into Germanic society and the
Frankish state. Indeed, so complete was the absorption that by
the tenth century the whole focus of the German polity had
shifted to the Saxon territories, and Saxon princes had come to
lead it in their capacity as Holy Roman Emperors. No sooner,
however, were the Saxon regions integrated into Romano-
Germanic Europe than the latter began to push out beyond
Saxony into the Slav lands across the Elbe. By the beginning
of the thirteenth century the drive to the east had ended in the

German conquest of the entire area between the Elbe in the west and the Vistula in the east, and between the eastern Baltic in the north and the Tyrolean passes into Italy in the south.

Considered as a military and political operation, the conquest was the work of princes and feudal 'bosses', men like Henry the Lion of Saxony. Its main objects, obviously, were to add to the power and glory of rulers, to establish new princely and knightly patrimonies and to acquire new lands capable of economic exploitation. The drive behind it, however, was not confined to princes and their military helpers. It owed much of its following and popular repute to its religious or missionary objectives. From its very beginning the conquest was presented as the 'Wendish crusade', a campaign against the Slav infidels; and the religious enthusiasm thus generated was sufficient to enlist the official support of the Holy See, and also to divert the activities of the Teutonic Order from the conquest of the Holy Land to the reputedly similar enterprise in Prussia.

As a result of these military and missionary activities the Slav area between the Elbe and the Oder came to be parcelled out among a number of German principalities, and the whole of its population was Christianized. But probably the most remarkable result of the eastward conquests was the mass settlement of German immigrants, more especially in the parts which in modern times comprised the principalities of Brandenburg, Mecklenburg, Pomerania and western Silesia.

In the process of the settlement, the indigenous Slav population was not fully replaced. Some Slav communities may have been expelled or exterminated, but the extent to which the land was denuded of its native population can be easily exaggerated. It has been argued with good reason that in certain transAlbingian regions, especially in Mecklenburg, the main core of Slav population survived the German conquest and some of the Slav princes, such as those of Mecklenburg-Schwerin, continued to rule in the guise of a German dynasty. In the eastmost of the regions, particularly in East Prussia, and in the southeastern territories of Silesia and Bohemia, the German settlement remained too thin to suppress the predominantly Slav character of civilization and speech; and even further west – a few miles from Berlin and in the neighbourhood of Leipzig – sermons were still preached in Slavonic languages in the eighteenth century. The main achievement of German colonization and settlement was not so much to displace the existing Slav population as to introduce a large additional stratum of peasant immigrants, and thereby to create a wholly new agrarian economy on land hitherto unoccupied or else occupied very sparsely.

This political and economic expansion was accompanied and may even have been preceded by the commercial activities of German merchants. Long before the Wendish crusaders crossed the Elbe, i.e. all through the tenth and early eleventh centuries, German merchants from the steadily developing regions of the Rhine and the Weser had begun to reach out to the eastern fringes of the Saxon empire and to trade across the Elbe. Certain transcontinental routes, well defined on the map and frequently referred to in sources, were established by the end of the tenth century. The best known of them, the Hellweg, led from Soest and Dortmund in Westphalia to such crossing-points on the Elbe as Bardowiek and Magdeburg. The merchants most active on these routes were the men of Cologne; and men of Cologne they had to be, since the Rhine valley and Cologne at its head were the hub of such interregional trade as western Germany then knew. But from the very outset merchants from Westphalia and from Saxony east of the Rhine, especially from the former, also had a growing share in the trade. By the end of the twelfth century they had come to overshadow the merchants of Cologne and the other more westerly regions of old Germany, both as merchants and as mercantile colonizers. It fell to them to lead the movement of urban immigration and settlement which accompanied the colonizing activities of princes, landlords and peasants.

In the end, the colonizing merchants wove a whole network of new German towns and routes connecting them. Most of the

83 Medieval merchants' houses in Toruń, which developed as a commercial centre during the period of German eastward expansion.

towns were strung out along the south coast of the Baltic, but important commercial centres, like Toruń (Thorn) on the Vistula, also grew up on inland sites well served by rivers and roads. At least one of the towns, Lübeck, originated as early as the end of the eleventh century as a trading station or 'factory', set up by German merchants within or alongside a pre-existing Slav town. To begin with, this particular 'factory' appeared to accommodate itself successfully to Slav rule and even to enjoy the protection of Slav princes. Before long, however, it turned to a colonizing offensive. In the late thirties of the twelfth century, Adolph of Holstein invaded the land and burned the city, and in 1143 the Germans of Lübeck formally constituted themselves into a German town of the same name. This cuckoo-like procedure was not, however, followed everywhere, for most German towns in the Baltic regions apparently originated in new settlements, or in new German quarters attached to older Slav nuclei. One of the latest and most important, located on the estuary of the Vistula, was the town of Gdańsk, which soon rose to a dominating position in the commerce of eastern Prussia and western Poland.

The effects of this urban colonization on the power structure of the north European economies will be discussed later. From the point of view of economic geography, with which we have been dealing so far, its effect was to open up and to develop a maritime connection between western and eastern Europe and thereby to merge into a single commercial area the hitherto self-contained *Verkehrsgebiete* of north-western and of central and eastern Europe.

In this merger the merchants were not the sole agents. To adopt a phrase from a later age, 'trade followed the flag'. As the German princes and landlords spread their rule to the east, they created the political prerequisites for German activity beyond the Elbe, and made it possible for the German merchants not only to sail unhindered along the coastal waters of the Baltic but also to establish permanent commercial settlements ('factories' and towns) in the interior.

The potentialities of the commercial settlements and their role in building up and sustaining the economic power of German merchants were reflected in their siting and the way they spread over the map. They were so placed as to form staging posts and entrepôts at regularly spaced points along the sea route and along the main inland routes to the sea. Most of them – above all Wismar, Rostock, Stettin and Gdańsk – were sited at places at which the north-flowing rivers of the German plain ran into the Baltic. Some, such as Reval, Riga or Dorpat, were seaports as well as administrative centres serving the Lat-

vian and Livonian possessions of the knightly Orders in the

eastern Baltic. In addition, the two most important towns on the route, the neighbouring cities of Hamburg and Lübeck, benefited not only from their location at the Baltic end of the Elbe valley, tapping the wealth of the newly opened-up Wendish hinterland, but also from their position at the foot of the Jutland peninsula.

As long as the maritime traffic to and from the west hugged the coasts and did not venture across the open seas, the Jutland peninsula was an impassable land barrier. Boats had to be unloaded at Hamburg on their way east and at Lübeck on their way west, and then carried across the peninsula and reloaded at the other side for a further voyage by water. In this way the two towns became unavoidable intermediaries in whatever traffic there was, and stood to benefit from all increases in the trade of other towns along the route. They derived advantages, too, from the great wealth of the fishing grounds off the nearby coast of southern Sweden (Skania), and were also able to draw on the wealth and importance of their Westphalian founder families. Thus favoured, Lübeck soon acquired a predominant role amidst other German towns trading to the Baltic, a role which eventually raised it to the position of the informal capital of the German Hanse.

84 Remains of an eleventh-century wooden boat found in Stettin, a member of the Hanseatic League from its inception.

Later in this essay I shall try to show how the new network of routes transformed the very composition of the trade, and thereby helped to reshape the economies of the regions it served. The trade flowing up and down the rivers and along the Baltic route was, to an ever-increasing extent, to consist of goods producible and consumable in quantities large enough and at prices low enough to rank as 'essentials'. The Germans trading in the Baltic and across central and eastern Germany, and only they, were able to sustain the flow of these goods and to control their sources and markets. This made them all but indispensable in both East and West, and opened to them positions of power at points well beyond the natural termini of the Baltic sea-lanes.

Within the regions still ruled by the Slavs, native princes and merchants had to direct their exports to places dominated by the German merchants. The town of Novgorod on Lake Ilmen, connected with the Baltic by a short water route, housed a German 'factory' dominating the trade of the town and drawing to itself the entire foreign trade of north-eastern Europe. Further south, the Russian towns of Smolensk, Pskov, Polotsk and Vitebsk, as well as others in Volhynia and Podolia, were not, like Novgorod, obviously dominated by German 'factories'. They nevertheless functioned as outlets through which Russian trade with Germany and the West was channelled. For their part Gdańsk and Toruń drew to themselves the bulk of the timber trade of eastern Poland and western Prussia.

The position of the German merchants in the West was for a time almost equally powerful. The essential commodities of eastern origin found large and expanding markets in western European countries. And as long as they were able to control the supply of these commodities, the German merchants were welcome and indeed irreplaceable, and were consequently able to obtain exclusive commercial privileges in several western countries. In most of these countries they established commercial 'factories' and trading stations, of which those of Bruges,

London and Bergen were the most important. Eventually their commercial activities brought them into Italy as well; and the *Fondaco dei Tedeschi* in Venice became very nearly the sole south European outpost of east-to-west trade.

In this way the Baltic route had, by the end of the thirteenth century, become the principal single artery of north European commerce, and thereby one of the main sinews of economic power in eastern Europe. However, this system of east-to-west connections and influences was not destined to survive long beyond the second half of the fourteenth century. In the first place, political and demographic changes gradually reduced the impetus of the German drive to the east. The political vacuum in the Slav lands, which had enabled the Germans to conquer and occupy the territories of the western Slavs in the earlier Middle Ages, was eventually filled by the rising power of the Slav states and in the first place by that of Jagiellonian Poland. In 1410 the political balance was finally redressed by the Polish victory over the Teutonic Order at Tannenberg.

The battle of Tannenberg put an end to German conquests, but even before this the German ability to fill the conquered territories with settlers had given out. The demographic pressure behind the flow of immigrants from western Germany and Flanders slackened in the fourteenth century and finally exhausted itself after the Black Death of 1348. As a result, the last eastern territories to be subjected to German political rule, such as eastern Silesia, Bohemia, Styria or the lake regions of eastern Prussia, were never fully Germanized. The Germans who had established settlements there by the early fourteenth century were not reinforced by later drafts of colonists, and thus remained for ever mere enclaves of a linguistic and ethnic minority.

The slackening of German expansion and colonization may or may not have reduced the actual volume of east-to-west trade (we do not possess sufficient evidence for measuring its turnover), but it certainly weakened the sway of the German merchants over it. And one of the reasons why this sway weakened is that the maritime route across the Baltic, and the land routes feeding it, were displaced in the course of the late fourteenth and fifteenth centuries, so losing their prime importance in east-to-west trade.

A striking feature in the economic geography of European trade in the late fourteenth and fifteenth centuries was the deflection of a large and a growing proportion of the trade away from the northernmost lanes. In this respect the changing role of the maritime lane across the Baltic was crucial. Recent historians of the Hanseatic League have raised objections to the tendency of some of their predecessors to build the whole history of north-western trade round the progress of the Baltic sea route and the towns along it. They rightly point out that the sea route was fed by the commercial currents flowing towards it from the interior, and that much, perhaps the bulk, of east European trade flowed between towns in the Baltic hinterland and along the trade routes traversing it in every direction. These objections notwithstanding, it is important, in considering the relations of eastern and western Europe, to bear in mind that throughout the Middle Ages waterways and especially sea-lanes were by far the cheapest and the best suited to movements of bulky and inexpensive goods. And since large quantities of such goods were the distinguishing characteristic of east–west trade in northern Europe, the importance of the Baltic route and the Baltic towns in long-distance trade was bound to be greater than that of land routes and land-bound towns further south. It was only in later centuries when, for reasons which were largely geo-political, the sea-borne trade was temporarily in decline, that the role of land routes and of the towns along them began to rival or even to exceed that of the Baltic Sea and the Baltic towns.

This phase of relative decline in the importance of the Baltic routes was ushered in by several changes along it, and in the first place by the *Umlandfahrt* – a newly opened sea route round the Jutland peninsula. With the new, wholly maritime, lane open to navigation, it was no longer necessary to reload cargoes at

Lübeck and Hamburg, and direct sea voyages from the Low Countries to the eastern Baltic, bypassing the two towns, became possible and profitable.

The principal beneficiaries of the change were the Dutch. Their industry and commerce and, above all, their shipping had greatly advanced in the course of the late fourteenth and fifteenth centuries. They were now proving themselves to be efficient sailors, highly competitive carriers and agents of entrepôt trade. They were able, therefore, to exploit the new opportunities on the route and to challenge the German monopoly of Baltic shipping. To a somewhat smaller extent the English also began to compete in the Baltic. Having in the course of the late fourteenth and early fifteenth centuries developed a cloth-making industry, they tried to trade with eastern Europe directly, carrying their cloth to the Baltic and fetching from there important return cargoes.

It was very largely in order to ward off this Anglo-Dutch threat, and to back up their threatened monopoly with political and naval action, that in 1367 the German towns, meeting in Stralsund to confer on their conflict with Scandinavia, converted their association, hitherto informal, into an overtly political organization: the Hanseatic League. As a political and naval power this League survived until well into the modern era, but it could not reverse the unfavourable trend of geopolitical change. The League's repeated attempts to beat down Dutch and English competition in the course of the fifteenth century merely succeeded, time after time, in destroying the peace on the high seas and thereby interrupting the flow of Baltic trade. Similarly, the Hanseatic attempts to enforce the League's monopoly in the West by repeated embargoes and boycotts, drove the trade away from centres in which the Germans were entrenched, especially Bruges, to centres not dominated by them, such as Antwerp. The northern route and its termini in most western parts of Europe were becoming less reliable and less important, and, as their importance declined, alternative routes developed.

The most important of the alternative routes was a variant (or variants) of the southerly overland routes which, as we have seen, ran across Germany and the countries of south-eastern Europe to Poland and south Russia. These southern routes grew in importance not only because merchants were anxious to escape the Hanseatic stranglehold over Baltic trade, but also because southern Germany was becoming increasingly prosperous. The towns of Nuremberg, Augsburg and Regensburg do not appear to have suffered from the fifteenth-century depression to the same extent as most of the towns of western Germany. For one thing, the mining and metallurgical industries of southern Germany, which these towns served and controlled, revived towards the end of the Middle Ages. In addition, the evidence suggests that the main trade routes to Italy shifted eastwards to the advantage of the near-lying towns of southern Germany. Thus favoured, these cities seem to have entered on that upward path which they were destined to tread so successfully in the sixteenth and seventeenth centuries.

There may also have been corresponding development in the Slav areas. South-western Poland may have been less affected by the general depression which, in the closing centuries of the Middle Ages, lowered the tempo of interregional trade elsewhere. Hence the rising importance of south Polish connections and of the towns of Lwow and Cracow which benefited from the southward shift of western routes and grew in economic importance to the detriment of the northern Slav termini and of the Baltic route.

THE NORTHERN ROUTE: THE COMMODITIES

The southwards shift of the east-to-west routes was a geographical and economic transformation whose direct and immediate consequences were reflected mainly in the fortunes and policies of the Hanseatic League and in the powers of German cities over the regions they controlled. What appeared to be at stake was, first and foremost, the prosperity and the economic role of Lübeck, Hamburg, Gdańsk and Bruges, and

85 The outside of a German mine in the late fifteenth century; from a woodcut by the Hausbuch Master ▶

the economic privileges which German merchants enjoyed in London, Scandinavia or the Low Countries. But, from the historical point of view, the most important results were the less conspicuous and more deeply hidden changes in the very composition of the trade which flowed along the great routes, both old and new. Indeed, the humdrum detail of the east-to-west traffic, i.e. of the commodities entering into it, holds the key to the proper understanding of the transformation which the trade wrought upon the economic system and social fabric of northern Europe.

The history of east-to-west trade, considered from the point of view of its material make-up, falls into several well-defined phases, roughly corresponding to those of its geo-political development. In its initial phase, that preceding the German expansion to the east, most of the commercial traffic of northern Europe to and from eastern Europe, like the trade of earlier centuries in southern Europe, was, from the purely economic point of view, supererogatory; that is to say, its commodities did not cater for the major needs of the regional economies and societies in either East or West. I have already pointed out that apart from slaves – and they were, so to speak, goods in transit – the western imports from the East consisted mostly of luxuries of eastern and Byzantine origin and were paid for partly by a few metal goods, such as weapons, and mainly in bullion.

In all probability both the quantity and the make-up of the commercial traffic between East and West changed in the initial phase of German expansion – the one which opened when the Saxon lands were conquered and absorbed, and the West-phalian and Saxon merchants appeared at the Elbe and its crossings. In that period trade was undoubtedly greater in volume than in the preceding epoch and probably brought both the West and the East a somewhat wider range of imports.

The eastern exports which, measured by value, must at that time have outweighed all the other commodities of eastern European origin, were furs. So far as we can gather from literary references and from pictorial representations, imported furs were articles of apparel ranking as semi-luxury: relatively expensive but widely used. Ordinary peasants protected themselves from the rigours of winter by humble sheepskins, but men of greater substance in villages and in towns could afford other and better furs; and invariably they bought them, wore them and transmitted them with the rest of their heirlooms. These furs were relatively costly and, above all, differed in their cost (one fifteenth-century document put the value of a coat of ermine at sixty times that of a comparable coat of red fox), and thus were not merely utilitarian and convenient for men living in severe climates but could also be employed as status symbols and as objects of ostentatious display. Men bought and wore furs to suit their rank and wealth; indeed, this display function of furs became so generally accepted that, in the fifteenth and sixteenth centuries, national and municipal authorities in England and elsewhere thought it fit to regulate the ranking of men by the furs they wore. For these and other reasons furs, though not strictly essential commodities, came to represent a large and expanding market and to absorb considerable material resources.

Little is known about other imports from eastern Europe during the period. By inference from later evidence it appears that certain products of eastern woodlands which were to figure in the trade of the fourteenth and fifteenth centuries, such as beeswax and possibly honey, had begun to come in from the East in the eleventh and the twelfth centuries. Other commodities about which we hear in later periods – Baltic amber or goose-feathers and down – may also have begun to cross the Elbe in the eleventh and the twelfth centuries. Yet, in total, the trade in such commodities as these, though larger in volume and value than articles of *grande luxe* imported in the previous centuries, still remained on the periphery of medieval existence and could not have made much difference to the fundamental processes of economic life.

It was only in the final phases of medieval east-to-west trade, those beginning at the very end of the twelfth century, that the merchants who were engaged in it commenced dealing to an increasing extent in bulky commodities which served the common needs of ordinary people and involved large volumes of material resources and great numbers of men in their production. The historical factors behind this transformation in the composition of east–west trade have already been indicated. In the first place, there was the opening up of the east European interior; in the second, the Baltic route. The newly reclaimed and settled interior of eastern Europe yielded new commodities of an essential nature; the Baltic route made it possible to move these commodities over large distances and to place them in markets separated from their sources by the whole breadth of two seas.

Most of the 'essential' commodities were raw materials and foodstuffs. The raw materials, like the beeswax which began to arrive during the preceding period, were largely sylvan products: the natural yield of the vast forests of eastern Europe. Some of them were, so to speak, 'processed' or 'semi-manufactured': pitch, tar and resin drawn from the coniferous trees, and potash which was made by burning wood. However, by far the most important of the sylvan products of eastern Europe was timber, much of it shipped to the West in 'semi-manufactured' form, as boards or wainscoting. In the fifteenth century some timber was also sent to the West in the fully manufactured form of boat-hulls or complete ships. Most of the timber, however, came to the West unmilled and unwrought. In general, Baltic timber won its position in trade as raw material for the constructional and shipbuilding industry of the Low Countries, north-west Germany and England.

So great were the forested areas of eastern Europe and so abundant were its reserves of timber, that the ability of the Baltic regions to supply large quantities of exportable timber is easily explained. Equally easy to account for is eastern Europe's accessibility to trade: the forest lands of eastern Germany and western Poland and Russia were traversed by rivers, flowing into the sea, along which cut timber could be floated easily and cheaply. And by this time, there was a ready market for eastern timber in the countries of western Europe. The traditional picture of life in medieval Germany and even in medieval England, as set out in Grimm's fairy tales or the story of Robin Hood – a land of forests harbouring wolves and outlaws – is largely myth. In actual fact the forest lands of thirteenth-century Europe had been greatly reduced in the course of the preceding five or six hundred years of internal reclamation and colonization. Some parts of western Europe, such as the uplands of south Germany and subalpine Swabia, Bavaria and Austria, or some areas in south-eastern and south-western France or the west midlands in England, still contained large areas of woodland. But in most other regions, especially those in which mixed farming prevailed, woodlands were now so small that usable timber was both scarce and very dear.

Moreover, it is doubtful whether domestic resources of timber would have met all western needs even had woodlands in the West remained intact. The characteristic home-grown timber of north-western Europe was the hardwoods, mainly oak and ash. They were valuable for many uses in building, shipbuilding and the manufacture of furniture and utensils. They were not, however, ideally suited for uses for which long poles, beams or struts were required. For these, softwoods were better, and for softwoods England, like much of the rest of western Europe, largely depended upon imports from regions where the pine and the yew grew well. When, at the end of the twelfth century, king John decided to construct a hunting-lodge in the heart of the Savernake forest, he apparently imported wood from Norway; and we must presume that he was not the only builder whose demand for timber could not be satisfied by the kind of oak which stood in the forest of Savernake.

In the twelfth century the softwoods needed in the West, as well as some other timbers, came mainly from Scandinavia. Specialized historical studies, such as Bugge's renowned book on the Norwegian timber trade, perhaps give a somewhat exaggerated picture of this trade; yet with all allowances made for the magnifying lens of the specialist, the fact remains that large quantities of timber were regularly shipped from Norway to England and that England was at that time greatly dependent on Norway for its supply of wood. It may well be that Scandinavian timber was somewhat less essential to other parts of western Europe. The timber of the south German woodlands may still have been floated down the Rhine and the Weser as it had been in the Dark Ages when that trade was in the hands of the Frisians. It is also possible that the south-western regions of France, or the French provinces bordering on Switzerland, or the parts of England along the Welsh marches, still disposed of sufficient supplies of home-grown timber as not to be greatly dependent on foreign supplies. But most other regions had to tap the reserves of woodland in Scandinavia or other forested regions of Europe to satisfy their most essential local needs.

The opening of the Baltic forest lands to westborne trade did not, therefore, signify the beginning of the European timber trade, but rather its diversion to sources beyond the Elbe. Thus diverted, the trade was destined to grow in size and importance. On *a priori* grounds it appears obvious that Baltic timber would not have ousted Norwegian had it not been cheaper; and we must assume that, being cheaper, it was more widely used and was bought and sold in larger quantities than the timber available to the West in earlier times. On the same assumption, it is also possible to argue that the abundance of cheap softwoods of high quality favoured the innovation in the construction of western ship-hulls – those of north European 'hulks' and 'cogs' – which preceded and prepared for the technological advances in the design and construction of boats at the close of the Middle Ages. If this is so, it might not be fanciful to suggest that the shift in the timber trade to the Baltic contributed, albeit obliquely, to the great progress in shipping, shipbuilding and sea transport which we associate with the age of discovery and with Dutch, Portuguese and English navigation in the sixteenth and the seventeenth centuries.

86 Timber haulers at work (c. 1500).

87 Medieval merchant ship.

The timber trade must also have had some impact on the economic activities of men in the Slav and east German forest lands. The timber had to be cut; some of it had to be worked and fashioned; all of it had to be floated to the sea. We know very little about the way in which this working and fashioning of timber was organized, or about the men employed in eastern Europe as woodcutters or shipwrights; and we have no direct means of estimating their numbers or their incomes. We have, however, a certain amount of evidence about river transport of timber and the manner in which it was conducted. In his classical treatise, now nearly a hundred years old, Theodore Hirsch described the rafts which were floated down the Russian and Polish rivers to Toruń and Gdańsk, so that we can at least imagine how medieval lumberjacks conducted their water-gypsy lives. The picture so imagined differs little from that of the west Russian lumber trade to the Baltic in the late nineteenth

159

century. The trade created a type of employment, and favoured a mode of life, which must have been very similar in all periods, though naturally the scale of the operation in western Russia at the end of the nineteenth century was greater than in the fourteenth and fifteenth centuries.

However, of the different commodities entering the Baltic trade, the one which affected economic and social development the most was not timber. In sheer volume and value, as well as in its impact on the indigenous economy, the trade in timber was eventually outstripped by that in grain. The growing of grain in sufficient quantities and at low enough costs to make bulk exports practical necessitated changes in agriculture which were bound to impress themselves deeply on the economic system as a whole. The activities of landlords, their relation to their tenants and labourers and, in a more general way, the condition of ordinary men, were intimately bound up with the fortunes of agriculture and thereby also with the development of exports.

Here again, some readers may wonder why any country in this period required and was able to absorb large imports of grain, and how producing countries managed to yield them. Was not medieval agriculture, and, indeed, the medieval economy in general largely self-sufficient? Did not the overwhelming majority of medieval producers practise subsistence farming, and was not the grain trade, for this reason alone, both small and intensely local? This picture of the medieval economy has, however, long been discarded. It is now well established that many households and regions in the Middle Ages did not produce enough to feed themselves, while others produced enough to provide surpluses. Indeed, so essential was the grain trade in medieval life that it appears to have formed the basis of the very pattern of regional settlement and regional specialization.

This was certainly true of Scandinavia. It is difficult to imagine that western Norway, so ill-suited to the production of cereals, would have been occupied by its Germanic settlers except on the presumption that grain, some grain, could be obtained from outside. Certainly, in the twelfth and thirteenth centuries Norway was greatly dependent on imports of food, and England was the main source of grain. A much-quoted speech of king Haakon Hakonsen in 1138 underlines how indispensable, and therefore how welcome, English imports and importers were at that time. Similarly, it is difficult to imagine how Frisian society could have established itself and subsisted on the wet sands and the inundated pastures of the Rhine estuary before the ninth century had it not been able to import grain from higher and drier lands. When in the twelfth and thirteenth centuries Flanders developed its relatively highly industrialized economy, and when in the late fourteenth and fifteenth centuries Holland did likewise, they had to rely on food imports, mainly from the grain-growing regions of the lower Seine. We also know that as Gascony and Poitou developed their viticulture and became Europe's largest wine-producing and wine-exporting regions, they also lost the

88 Making wine. The grapes are picked, tasted by a noble couple, put into a barrel to be trodden underfoot and finally pressed. From a late fifteenth-century tapestry of the Loire valley.

161

ability to feed themselves and had to import large quantities of grain, which in the late fourteenth and fifteenth centuries came mainly from or via England.

It would seem, therefore, that what the Baltic trade achieved was not the creation for the first time in the Middle Ages of an interregional grain trade, but rather a change in the geographical distribution of what had always been an important commercial commodity. Instead of coming from the middle Rhine valley or Picardy or England, the grain for Europe's deficient regions now began to come from eastern European plains opened up in the process of colonization east of the Elbe. In Scandinavian countries German imports displaced English grain, and German grain-importers became indispensable and hence also powerful. Above all, Flanders, and later the northern Netherlands (modern Holland), began to take their grain imports from the Baltic regions.

Moreover, the Baltic supplies were so abundant and reliable – and possibly also so cheap – that they were also shipped to places which did not regularly require imports of foodstuffs but were capable of putting cheap grain to other uses. In the later Middle Ages Hamburg developed a flourishing brewing industry based on corn imported from the Baltic; and in the fifteenth century Baltic grain also enabled the northern Netherlands to develop their brewing. Generally speaking, the economic growth and prosperity of the northern Netherlands in that century would have been impossible without regular supplies of Baltic grain. It is also probable that Baltic grain was shipped or trans-shipped to Bordeaux from Gdańsk in years in which English output was insufficient to supply Gascony.

Directly and indirectly, Baltic cereals were available to swell supplies of grain all over Europe and make up for its deficiencies at times when, and places in which, harvests fell short of requirements. It would not, therefore, be fanciful to suggest that availability of Baltic supplies may have been one of the reasons, albeit a subsidiary one, why grain prices all over Europe were relatively low in the late fourteenth and fifteenth

89, 90 Left, sixteenth-century salt storehouses in Lübeck dating originally from medieval times. Below, sixteenth-century half-timbered granary in Geislingen, Germany.

centuries and why they were even sagging gently in the four or five decades before 1480.

The return cargoes, with which the westerners paid for Baltic goods, were not perhaps as indispensable as Baltic grain, but they were nevertheless bulk imports and were destined to be consumed in large quantities. The bulkiest and the most indispensable of the western imports to the East was salt, the principal food preservative and the principal raw chemical in the Middle Ages. To begin with, most of the salt shipped east came from the area of Lüneburg, west of the Elbe, and was shipped mainly from Hamburg. Lüneburg salt, however, was eventually displaced by the cheaper and more readily available salt of the Bay of Biscay (or, to be more exact, the Bay of Bourgneuf). In the fifteenth century, the great Bay fleets, sometimes made up of more than a hundred ships, regularly

163

sailed with cargoes of salt from the west coast of France, past the
Low Countries, to the herring fisheries off the south coast of
Sweden (Skania) and off the north coast of Holland, and then
beyond the Jutland peninsula to Gdańsk and even to Novgorod.

The Bay fleets also carried miscellaneous industrial goods of
western manufacture, as did all ships trading with the Baltic. By
far the most important of the manufactured goods was, of
course, cloth. The imported cloth was very expensive by comparison with native linen textiles, or even with the coarser
woollens made locally. Nevertheless, the quantities which
could be absorbed by eastern European markets, including
those of Russia, were very large; and eastern Europe consequently became one of the main outlets for the western
European cloth industry.

At first, the bulk of the imported cloth came from Flanders.
It was, as a rule, bought by German merchants in Bruges, and
taken by them to the Baltic towns, from where it was distri-

buted all over eastern Europe. At the end of the fourteenth century, however, the Flemish cloth industry declined, and that of England and Holland largely replaced it in the eastern markets. Some, perhaps most, of this cloth was also handled by Hanseatic importers, but throughout the fifteenth century the English and the Dutch, especially the former, tried to keep the marketing of their cloth in their own hands.

Most of the conflicts between England and the Hanseatic League, of which there were several in the fifteenth century, arose over the attempts of English merchants to establish themselves as importers of cloth in the Baltic area, more particularly in Gdańsk. To begin with, these attempts failed. Political conditions in England at the time of the Wars of the Roses were too unstable to provide English merchants with the political support they needed. The final defeat in the Hundred Years War also had a debilitating effect on England's political and

92 A careful record was kept of trading activities: an early fourteenth-century trade book from Nuremberg records the sale of Flemish cloth.

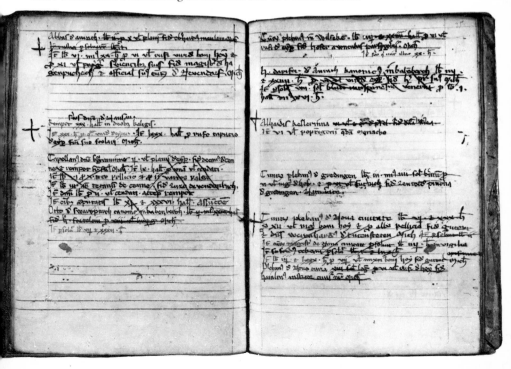

naval power. Thus favoured, the Hanseatic League was able, for the time being, to smother English ambitions in the Baltic. But in the sixteenth century the greater political influence and naval power of the Tudor state, and the retreat of the Germans in Gdańsk and East Prussia before the advancing power of the Poles, enabled England to revive her ambitions in the Baltic and to pursue them more successfully than before. Earlier still, the Dutch had fought successfully for their share in Baltic shipping and trade. In this way the cloth exports from western Europe to the East contributed to the geo-political changes of the fifteenth century which I have already described.

By comparison with salt and cloth, the other western exports were much less important. Metal goods of every kind came from Cologne and eastern Flanders, mostly Liège. Wine came from Burgundy and Gascony; cow hides, sheepskins, tin and pewter came from England; and (possibly) herring came from Swedish and later from Dutch fishing grounds.

In retrospect, however, even these important return cargoes did not have economic and social repercussions as far-reaching as exports from the east, and especially the flow of east European grain. If the adjective 'colonial' has any relevance to European conditions at the end of the Middle Ages, the export of cereals is one, perhaps the only, branch of trade which can conceivably be so classified: not only was it confined to unprocessed agricultural produce, i.e. grain and not malt or beer or flour, but it was largely paid for with manufactured imports; moreover, it was in the hands of outsiders, west European merchants and shippers, and it subjected the fortunes, the economic organization and social structure of eastern economies to the requirements of western markets. There is little doubt that the grain trade, as it developed at the close of the Middle Ages and in the early centuries of the modern era, had an impact on economic conditions and social relations in eastern regions comparable to the impact of modern international commerce on under-developed countries exporting primary produce. To this impact we shall now pass.

Eastern Europe diverged widely from the West in its economic and social development. It would have diverged even if it had been unaffected by trade, since its economy and society were a product of recent conquest, immigration and new settlement. In any event, dissimilarities were not levelled out by east-west trade; on the contrary, the commercial exchanges between the two halves of Europe widened the economic and social divergence. The divergence had only begun to reveal itself by the end of the Middle Ages, but in some parts of eastern and central Europe it was already well under way by the end of the fifteenth century. But in its medieval beginnings, as in its more modern phases, it derived much of its momentum from the pressures generated by trade.

In the early stages of German conquest and settlement the societies of West and East differed in detail and degree rather than in substance, more especially at their topmost levels. At these levels social structure conformed, broadly speaking, to what is now generally recognized as the feudal order. The role which the upper ranks of society in eastern Europe, mainly the owners of estates, were called upon to play in central and local government was in essence the same as that played by owners of fiefs in western Europe during the earlier centuries of the Middle Ages. The eastern European landowners, like the landed knights and nobility in the West, were a military class *par excellence*; and as such they bore the main burden in the conquest and occupation of the new territories. In the new territories, once they had been occupied and settled, the landowners as a rule continued to perform the military and administrative functions appropriate to members of the upper ranks of society. To this extent, the structure of state economy and society in the eastern half of Europe may be said to be 'feudal' in the broadest sense of the term.

Nevertheless, eastern feudalism differed in several important respects from that in most western countries. It was less hierarchical than in certain parts of southern France (or, indeed, than in the Holy Land), and in some parts of the East it was more anarchical, less subordinated to the central power and less easily controlled by it. The duties, obligations and local powers of the noblemen and knights were not solely dependent upon an implied feudal contract between them and their suzerains (by no means all the large estates were in fact held on terms identical to those of western fiefs); rather, they sprang from their *de facto* positions as soldiers, owners of land and colonizing *entrepreneurs*. As we shall see presently, this *de facto* feudalism may in later centuries have allowed individual landlords a freedom of action and opportunities for the exercise of their power which were all the greater for not being bound by the terms of an implied feudal contract.

Considerably greater were the differences in the conditions of lower men in the two halves of Europe. Everywhere in western Europe the manorial ties between landlords and peasant tenants were dissolving during the twelfth and the early thirteenth centuries. Larger numbers of manorial tenants saw their personal liberties enlarged and the burdens of their services and obligations lightened. In this way they were gradually approaching the condition of freeholders. Nevertheless, in the twelfth century this process had not yet been completed in most places; and except for relatively small groups of free peasants holding by allodial tenure, most peasants in western Europe still lived and held their lands in conditions of manorial dependency of some sort or another. Moreover, though the legal position of manorial peasants – their personal status and their tenurial obligations – was improving during the twelfth century and was to improve more radically still in the fourteenth and fifteenth centuries, their material level of life was low and sinking. Their poverty was due to purely physical causes, mainly the pressure of population. The ratio of land to hands and mouths was unfavourable, and peasant holdings were small. In most parts of Europe, they were also becoming smaller as population increased and as reserves of reclaimable land dwindled.

By comparison, the condition of peasants in the East, especially the German immigrants, was much superior; it was freer, more prosperous, and seemingly more promising. In many places the trend was set not by German immigrants but by Flemish settlers. The Flemings were Europe's pioneers in land reclamation and above all, in the draining and management of swampy lands; they were therefore sought after by the organizers of east European colonization and attracted to the East by allurements of every kind. In the twelfth century Flemish peasants, unlike those of most other parts of France or England, were personally free and held land by wholly free titles; and they had to be offered conditions of tenure equally free if they were to be enticed to the East. The total number of Flemings thus persuaded to move was probably quite small, but the Flemish version of free status and free tenure was also made available to the bulk of German immigrants. In order to attract settlers, landlords and colonizing entrepreneurs promised and gave the German peasant settlers land to be held by 'Flemish law'.

Equally important was the quantity and quality of land made available to them. Land, and above all land recently reclaimed and thus unexhausted, was less scarce than in the West. Average holdings were large by comparison with average holdings in Franconia, Swabia or Westphalia, from where most of the immigrants had come. In this way, in eastern Germany and in the other Slav lands where new immigrants predominated, a prosperous as well as a free peasant society was emerging.

In reality actual development proceeded in a diametrically opposite direction. In the West, especially in England and France, the hold of the feudal landlords over state and society weakened as national governments consolidated themselves and as commerce expanded; in the East the power of the estate owners grew, while the peasants were brought to the very threshold of enslavement and impoverishment. In most parts of eastern and central Europe, the threshold was not passed until the sixteenth and seventeenth centuries. But in some parts, especially in the eastern fringes of Germany, such as the march of Brandenburg, it was approached very closely in the late fifteenth century.

The divergence between East and West was rooted in the origin of the eastern European states. From their beginnings, the princely states of eastern Europe differed from their western prototypes, though the differences were not mainly economic or social in origin, but political and constitutional. According to the commonly held view, the feudal landlords in western Europe established their power in the Dark Ages and increased it subsequently at the expense of the state and the princely authority, only to lose it in later centuries as and when princely powers and the authority of the state grew. This generalization may not be universally applicable. In some countries, such as England or Normandy and some of the principalities of France, the feudal order was, so to speak, 'nationalized'; it was adopted by the English kings, the Norman dukes and the kings of Norman Sicily as an instrument of their own authority, above all as an orderly system of military service and local administration. However, by degrees, in the course of the twelfth and thirteenth centuries in England, and at somewhat less clear-cut points of time in France, the feudal hierarchy was ceasing to be the principal instrument of state government. The latter began to rely instead on civil servants and hired soldiers for the military, administrative and judicial services it required.

In the German principalities beyond the Elbe and in Prussia the government depended, from the very outset, on the support and services of its landowning knights and nobles – the *Junkers* as they eventually came to be known – for the exercise of its essential functions, and this dependence increased in the later centuries. The attempts by Ivan the Terrible of Russia in the sixteenth century to end the dependence of the state on the ancient nobility and to govern through the *Oprichina* – a retinue of servants and police agents under the tsar's personal command – succeeded for a time in imposing upon the country a type of autocratic despotism. But it did not outlast Ivan's reign and after him the new monarchy in Russia called into being a land-owning class on which it could base its authority, and from which it could draw its officers and administrators. In Poland, relations between the state and its landowners evolved somewhat differently. For one thing, the great magnates played an increasingly important role and the powers of the state progressively weakened in the course of the early centuries of the modern era. But in the late Middle Ages, and to some extent even later, the Polish monarchy had to draw on the landed estate and the landowning nobility for the machinery and the personnel of its administration and army.

The resurgence of feudalism, however, was clearest in the east German principalities. There, in the course of the later Middle Ages and the early centuries of the modern era, the powers of the feudal landowners grew. The principalities stood in great need of military service. They were, after all, frontier states; they administered and defended territories which were large and comparatively sparsely settled by medieval standards. Yet their administrative and military resources, above all their human cadres, were relatively meagre. In the absence of an old and powerful middle class, or of other nuclei of local power, the estates and their *Junker* owners were the only reserves of authority on which the state could draw, and whose loyalty it had to keep.

This loyalty had to be kept, and services to the state had to be paid for, as they had been in the initial phases of western feudalism and in Tsarist Russia, by grants of land and by facilities for its profitable exploitation. In the conditions of eastern Europe, the means of exploitation were at least as important as the land itself, since the latter was relatively abundant and estates were, to begin with, easily carved out. But as long as population remained scarce, there were few hands to turn the land to use. Ownership of land did not, therefore, give sufficient remuneration in itself. In the initial phases of colonization the most remunerative use for land was to settle it with people, and greater powers over other men were not what landowners

171

needed in order to attract peasant settlers. In these conditions a society of free and prosperous peasants was wholly compatible with the interests of landlords. But the value of land to the landlord, and its use by him, changed when colonization ceased and the corn trade developed. The large and growing market for grain offered great opportunities to owners of land for its profitable use. In eastern Germany and western Poland conditions were more favourable for the production of grain on a large scale and in large units than anywhere else at the end of the Middle Ages. Large corn-growing estates were thus becoming increasingly valuable provided they could be worked, i.e. provided men could be found to work them.

Thus it became the policy of *Junkers* to obtain as much good land as possible and as many labourers as were needed to cultivate it. Much of the better land was already in the possession of peasant cultivators; hence, the acquisition of peasant land became the policy of profit-conscious landowners. Similarly, the peasants were the only possible source of manpower for working on the land. So far as we know, in the early phases of colonization the number of smallholders or landless men willing to hire themselves to other men was very small. After the middle of the fourteenth century, when immigration petered out and population ceased to grow, or perhaps even began to decline, workers on the land became scarcer still, or, at least, more difficult to replace.

Hence the *Bauernlegen* (the 'laying of peasants'): a double-headed weapon to match the twin purposes it served. Peasant land was seized by landlords for additional arable cultivation; peasants were deprived of their holdings or had their holdings reduced in order to compel them to work as labourers. The compulsion to work could be clothed in legal forms. The so-called *Gesindezwang*, a compulsory service for peasants as labourers, frequently received the sanction of law, and could be enforced in courts. Other disabilities of a semi-servile character, restricting the peasant's freedom of movement and his status as the lords' equal in law, were also imposed on large

93 The church was one of the most powerful landowners in medieval Germany. In this miniature from an inventory of land taken by the monastery of Eichstätt in Bavaria (1497–1503), a nobleman, a burgher and a peasant are given plots of land in fief.

sections of the peasant population. In this way the peasants in eastern Germany at the end of the fifteenth and in the sixteenth century (and in Poland and Russia at a somewhat later period) moved from freedom to serfdom at the very time when western society was shedding most of the constraints of medieval serfdom.

The divergence was thus complete and appeared to be irreversible. It was not, however, the result of spontaneous economic change; it was brought about by the exercise of

173

landlords' power. Their influence and personal connections in the seats of central authority and the willingness of the central government to serve their interests, precluded any princely opposition to *Bauernlegen*, or any policies in defence of peasants comparable to the anti-enclosure measures of the Tudor government in England.

Consequently, the *Junkers* were able to turn to account their great and increasing powers in central and local government and in the judiciary. This might have happened even if the corn trade had failed to develop: the *Junkers* might still have conceived it in their interest, and found it in their power, to reduce the free peasants to serfdom. They did so in Russia in the seventeenth and eighteenth centuries even though Russian exports of grain at that time were as yet negligible. Nevertheless, there is no denying that the main reason why the *Bauernlegen* occurred in the other parts of eastern Europe earlier is that corn-trade exports were growing and appeared capable of further growth, and that landlords could not exploit the full potentialities of the trade so long as peasants owned much of the arable land and withheld their labour.

In this way one of the most tragic paradoxes of European history came to be enacted. In conventional histories, trade is often represented as a liberating force and as a solvent of serfdom and of feudal power: in this particular instance it enhanced the forces of resurgent feudalism. Trade is also said to be the great international leveller, capable of reducing the economic differences between regions and nations and extending common principles of social and economic organization. But at the close of the Middle Ages, and still more in the two subsequent centuries, the corn trade widened the differences between the economy and society of the East and those of the West. Indeed, in the end it created along the river Elbe one of Europe's sharpest lines of social and economic demarcation. And yet, as the essay which follows will show, this economic and social dividing-line occurred within the limits of a single European civilization.

# V CULTURAL INTERCHANGES
*Alexander Gieysztor*

In the earlier parts of this volume the course of political relation-
ships between East and West, particularly the confrontation
between the Germanic peoples and the Slavs, has been high-
lighted for the reader, as well as the economic development of
the east European peoples and the impact of religion and the
Catholic and Orthodox churches. It has been shown how all
were affected by the interconnections, peaceful and warlike,
between eastern and western Europe, and also by their counter-
actions. In conclusion, the reader is entitled to a study of
intellectual attitudes – that is to say, to some insight into the
whole movement of Slav civilization as it is refracted in the
consciousness of the men of the Middle Ages and in the specific
reality of the continued confrontation of eastern Europe and
the West.

Such a survey would easily become overloaded, if it were
taken literally, or too vague, if one were to be content with a
few general observations. We shall therefore single out for
examination three specific phases, or what may be called three
cultural crossroads of the Middle Ages, reached in the first place
by the western Slavs, and shall attempt to demonstrate the
changes in style of life, in social psychology, and in the collective consciousness of the different Slav peoples, as reflected in
literary and artistic sources, which each phase registers.

The first of the three turning-points, which we shall call pre-
Romanesque, extends over those few generations who built up
the great states – in Moravia, in Russia, in Poland and in
Bohemia – in the ninth, tenth and eleventh centuries. This was
a period of rapid and conscious acculturation, of willing acceptance of western models or of Slav adaptation of Byzantine

models. The second phase coincides with Romanesque humanism in the West; it continues in Poland and Bohemia during the
thirteenth century, whereas in Russia, committed to Mediterranean tradition through the medium of Byzantium, cultural
growth was interrupted by the Mongol invasion, and foreign
contacts were restricted to the commerce of Novgorod the
Great. The third phase, Gothic this time, began in Bohemia in
the fourteenth century, reached Poland in the fifteenth century,
and extended from there into the grand duchy of Lithuania
(ethnically Russian for the most part); it was characterized by a
greatly increased accessibility of the people to· the creation and
utilization of cultural wealth.

## CULTURAL ORIGINS: PRE-ROMANESQUE

Before describing further the features of the first conjuncture
we have just mentioned, let us see what was the starting-point
of the Slav civilizations before the decisive changes which led
them to that appropriation of cultural values, western or
Byzantine, which were thereafter to characterize their society
and institutions.

A comparative study of these civilizations and of that of
other peoples, such as the Scandinavians or the Balts, who
joined the great European family at approximately the same
time, would soon demonstrate that all started off from a more
or less similar cultural level, and showed a similar receptivity
to external influences. When we first encounter the Slavs they
already have an agricultural economy of long standing and an
established social system of territorial communities, clans and
tribes. The structure and vocabulary of their spoken language is
evidence of their cultural progress; for even before the great
migrations of the fifth, sixth and seventh centuries, it was
capable of expressing the phenomena of nature and society, and
of man's inner life, in a mature, sophisticated way. The Slav
peoples, in other words, had reached a stage at which they were
capable of adjusting to the values which reached them from
176     abroad at a time when social and political conditions were

94, 95, 96 Above left, silver earrings from Stará Kourim in Bohemia. Below left, silver chalice, probably Rhenish, found in a tomb near Kolin, Bohemia. The import of western *objets d'art* into eastern Europe flourished in the tenth century. Below, spurs and a girdle clasp *in situ* at the feet of a human skeleton in Mikul-čice, Moravia.

favourable to such an assimilation. The medieval state, the surest guarantor of ethnic and cultural identity, and of the particular political institutions of its people, was the main instrument of an acculturation which was effective though sometimes painful.

We purposely employ the term 'acculturation', much used today by sociologists dealing with developments in the Third World, where the historian is surprised to find so many analogies with medieval Europe. When it is a question of medieval Russia, Poland, Bohemia or Hungary, this term helps us to understand, and very often to demythologize our conceptions of, the origins of political consciousness, initially tribal, and then supra-tribal or even national, and to evaluate the activities of the state in furthering economic development and fostering civilization.

Political developments between the middle of the ninth century and the first decades of the eleventh century – that is to say, the rise of organized states in Moravia, Russia, Poland and Bohemia – were particularly conducive to a rapid acculturation and acceleration of cultural growth. The dynamism of the new political and social order created, first of all, violent contrasts in style of life, in the use of income, as well as in dress, eating habits, and amusements, between the privileged classes and the rest of the population. The fortified dwellings erected by the Moimirids in Moravia, the first Přemyslids in Bohemia, the Piasts in Poland, and the Varangian rulers in Russia – a dynasty Scandinavian in origin but assimilated by the Slavs from the tenth century – acted as centres which mustered together the ruling classes, their families, servants and followers. The machinery of the state accumulated production surpluses which previously had been dispersed over the countryside. It amassed them to satisfy the needs of the ruling class, which partly consumed them on the spot and partly exported them in return for luxury articles or precious metals. From the beginning the needs of the nobility had stimulated local production, gradually imposing on it a more efficient organization of more extended dimensions. By increasing the variety of consumer demands, the rulers thus initiated more varied forms of production and gave it new cultural patterns and content.

At first glance, it would seem that the ruling class – hardly more than a few dozen families, established at the princely courts of Kiev, Prague or Gniezno, or travelling with the ruler's household, or dispersed in provincial strongholds – alone participated in this cultural revolution. Recent archaeological investigations, however, have produced more precise information for ninth-century Moravia. These investigations have uncovered cemeteries in places which were the seats of Moravian power, and those at Staré Město are of particular interest. What they reveal is that only 1·6 per cent of the tombs contain rich gold ornaments of Byzantine and local origin; 29 per cent contain other, more modest objects; 10 per cent have only a single knife, and the rest – that is, rather more than half – contain no objects which establish definite social or cultural evidence. What sort of society does this evidence picture? Two per cent of nobles, 30–40 per cent of warriors and functionaries attached to their courts, or free peasants at various levels of affluence, and over 50 per cent of the population still unaccounted for, or enslaved?

These statistics should be regarded with caution, if only because of the pre-urban character of the Moravian fortified dwellings, very rare in a country where scattered rural homesteads predominated. On the other hand, the percentage of nobles arrived at in this way seems noteworthy since the proportions in better-known medieval societies are similar. Bearing in mind what is known of the population of central and eastern Europe of this time, 2 per cent of nobles of the Polish governing class at the time of its emergence around the year 1000, for example, would amount to some 4,000 families in round numbers. At first sight this may seem an unrealistically large number for the ruling aristocracy; but it is also possible that the figure indicates the advent of a new leisured class, forerunner of the provincial knights and noblemen of later times. 179

The high aristocracy in the prince's entourage, and the new social stratum which grew up around it, began to feel the need to assimilate foreign influences, adopting foreign ways and habits in order to increase their prestige. Foreign innovations such as stone buildings, hitherto unknown, or the import of works of art from abroad, exercised a subtle influence over the behaviour of the aristocratic class. They felt that in this way they were achieving equality of status and of cultural level with similar groups in post-Carolingian Europe, particularly in the Ottonian empire, which sent out missions as far as distant Kiev (though without positive results) and exercised an undoubted cultural influence on the duchies of Bohemia and Poland, and on the Hungarians, in the second half of the tenth century. The necessity for a higher authority, scarcely perceived during the tribal period, became more and more apparent and created the need for new ways to express it. This is seen in the early palaces and chapels, still few in numbers and small and modest in size, of which the vestiges have been recovered by archaeological research in Bohemia, Poland and Hungary. It is seen also in the rare traces of literary activity, hagiography and annals. Sparse and fragmentary though they are, these sources at least give us a glimpse of the contacts established in the tenth century by the ruling circles of eastern Europe with those countries which lay in the West.

The centres these circles sought out in the West were cities such as Liège, the 'Athens of the North' at the time of bishop Notger, Regensburg, St Gallen, Cologne, Trier and Rome. There they found teachers, and they knew how to choose them while preserving their own cultural and ethnic characteristics and independence of political action. We know the names of some of these 'instructors in civilization', such as the first German or Italian bishops at Prague or at Poznań, the Italian abbot Tuni, 'sly as a fox, and loved for this by his lord', Boleslav the Bold, or Bruno of Querfurt, a Saxon attracted by the Polish programme of missionary expansion, and its convinced spokesman at the court of the German king. Others whose

97, 98 Left, gold pitcher from the ninth-century treasure of Nagyszentmiklós, Hungary; probably Sassanian, it was originally owned by the Magyar Arpads. Below, grave hoard from Borucin, Poland, including silver buttons and a chain, buried in the first half of the eleventh century.

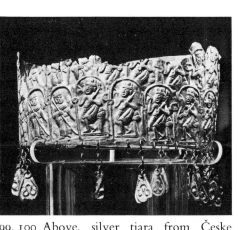

99, 100 Above, silver tiara from České Budejovice, Bohemia (*c.* 1100). Right, growing national consciousness: a group of Bohemians (*Boemenses*) appear (bottom right) on this Augustinian manuscript (*c.* 1200).

intellectual activity widened the scope of the cultural imagination of the ruling class have been forgotten.

The raising of the Czech duchy of Boleslav I, or the Polish duchy of Mieszko I, to a level which reflected the normal standards of aristocratic life at the time, and which no longer struck foreigners as backward, was the result of a conscious acceptance of models offered by the West, and of their adaptation to local needs and conditions. It was greatly aided by another contingency, economic this time – namely, the short burst of transcontinental and Baltic commerce between the middle of the ninth century and the first decades of the eleventh century. The states engaged in this trade in luxury goods, timber and other forest products and slaves, had large stocks of precious metals at their command, and when necessary were prepared to dispose of these to make purchases and investments which enhanced their prestige.

What were the circumstances that prevented this upsurge from being merely an episode which isolated the ruling class from the rest of the population culturally and racially? In fact, this did occur sometimes, among certain of the west Slav peoples. The duchy of the Obodrites, for example, when it finally attempted, too late, to modernize itself in the twelfth century, was unable to absorb western institutions and Christianity; it saved the native noble class and the ruling dynasty – the dynasty which, under the name of Mecklenburg-Schwerin and Mecklenburg-Strelitz, was not dethroned until 1918 – but only at the cost of rapid Germanization. The ordinary people, on the other hand, went under.

But the situation was different in Poland, Bohemia, Hungary and, in somewhat different circumstances, in Kievan Russia. In none of these countries did the influx of foreign institutions or evangelization (initially very superficial) by foreign clergy prevent the establishment of monarchies which played an independent role in international politics and the creation of states which represented distinct ethnic entities. One of the incentives which impelled the builders of these states, the

182

Přemyslids in Bohemia, the Piasts in Poland and St Stephen of Hungary, towards radical solutions, was their awareness of the need to create supra-tribal links, with the help of foreign models; and it is clear that for a long period it was only the inner circle of political leaders that was alive to this need. The fundamental fact they were able to rely on, in Bohemia and Poland – and even in Hungary, in spite of its lack of racial cohesion due to the conquest of the Slav territory by the Magyars – was that the overwhelming majority of the population spoke a common language. Once the states were organized, their very existence facilitated a standardization of terminology and linguistic usage, and political integration was quickly followed by the emergence of a common name to unite the various tribes. People began to think and speak of 'Bohemia', 'Polonia', 'Hungaria', as well as the native terms for the different tribal units.

On the other hand, there is reason to emphasize the remarkable degree of social mobility which characterized the first states in this part of Europe. The possibility of promotion from one social class to another, by service in the administrative and military organization of the growing monarchies, facilitated access to a higher level of civilization. Archaeological evidence enables us to observe the improvement of standards of living and of possibilities of satisfying them, among the broad masses of the population. It shows us the stages (the two most important fall in the middle of the tenth and towards the end of the eleventh century) in the creation of better material conditions: better constructed houses, improvements of diet, flourishing of the minor arts. Cultural self-identification, then, was the foundation of the first efflorescence, and of its whole subsequent evolution.

The second principal feature, which also lasted a long time, was the preference for the West – at least in Bohemia, Poland and Hungary – when organizational and institutional models were needed. Anxious to speed up the development of their countries, the ruling classes turned for guidance to European civilization in its western or Latin form. In all these countries western models played the main role at the height of the Middle Ages, and they proved far more dynamic than Byzantine civilization and its derivatives. In contrast with ninth-century Moravia, hesitating between Byzantium and the Slavonic rite on the one hand, and Bavaria and the Latin rite on the other, Bohemia opted speedily for the solution which the proximity of Bavaria forced upon it. The significance of the Slavonic rite, introduced into Moravia by Cyril and Methodius, and of Slavonic hagiography, is extremely controversial. It is sufficient here to say that their impact, either as a direct heritage from Moravia, or as a resurgence coming from Bulgaria or Dalmatia in the tenth or eleventh century, was limited to a few centres in Bohemia, such as the abbey of Sázava, founded in 1032 and dissolved in 1095. In southern Poland the traces of the Slavonic rite are minimal, although the Poles of the tenth century were not forced to opt for the West by political pressure or geographical proximity. Nevertheless they also quickly adopted western Christianity, immediately after the Czechs, and shortly before the Hungarians. This choice of western models did not mean exclusivity. The Czech, Polish and Hungarian states, bound together by dynastic ties and linked by dynastic marriages with Russia, the Elbe Slavs and Scandinavia, kept up contacts of all sort with their neighbours. Poland traded with the Slav and Viking Baltic, and also participated in the commerce along the east–west trade route which passed through Polish and Bohemian territory, linking Russia with the West, and extending via Hungary to Byzantium.

The third feature to delineate is the social order. The princes used the western civilizing elements as an instrument in their work of social and political consolidation. At first these influences affected mainly the upper ranks of society, the narrow circle formed by the prince and his entourage, and the result was therefore to separate them to a certain extent from the existing native culture. But gradually, as the old tribal links broke down, western elements were assimilated more generally into the system of administration and became the backbone of the social

101, 102 Below, capital from the Romanesque cathedral of St Adalbert in Esztergom (eleventh century), influenced by Lombard sculpture. Right, St Martin's rotunda, built on the Vyšehrad by Vratislav II (second half of the eleventh century).

structure. As Christianity slowly took root in Bohemia in the ninth and at the beginning of the tenth century, in Poland after 966, and in Hungary from the close of the tenth century, the values it brought with it helped to shape the social hierarchy, consolidating the existing class differences by an alliance between the existing political authority and the Catholic church which, however universal it may have been in some respects, was quick to adapt itself to the needs and framework of the local establishment.

There is no better witness to this process of cultural assimilation than the churches built in Bohemia, Poland and Hungary at this period. The round church of St Guy in Prague, the first cathedral of St Peter at Poznań, and the cathedral of St Adalbert at Esztergom, are monuments to the efforts made by these states to assimilate, by all available means, the Christian and monarchic vision of the world. They also forged a link with the most active cultural centres of the period – northern Italy and the Dalmatian coast, the Rhineland, Lorraine and Bavaria –

185

103 Eleventh-century silver bowl, stylistically a genuine product of Polish Romanesque art but relying in technique and iconography on Sassanian sources. The narrative cycle consists of scenes from the Biblical story of Gideon liberating the Hebrews.

from which they learned the forms of western art and obtained a supply of foreign craftsmen and of *objets d'art*. But this period also was marked by an increasing flow of native artistic production, the output of local craftsmen, which served the country more and more widely, side by side with the more sophisticated artistic achievements, as a sort of everyday art; here, too, foreign influence is seen in the adoption of figurative motifs, of which the Slavs, who belonged to the great zone of geometrical decoration, had made very little use up to that time.

Contacts with the outside world and the consequent social changes provoked tension between the simpler and more primitive way of life which the western Slavs had experienced while living in rural settlements in the shelter of the forests, and the new forms which developed in the following period. In spite of revolts and reversions to paganism, such as occurred in Bohemia in 929 and in Poland in 1038–39, a favourable political climate made it possible to resolve this tension in such a way that

the new cultural level was maintained and the work of acculturation and social reconstruction carried further, particularly in the
upper ranks of society around the rulers.

What part did Russia play in the contacts of the Slavs with
the West? Much was written of Russia and her riches in the
West, in *chansons de geste*, in chronicles and in geographical
treatises. She was linked with the West by far-flung dynastic
marriages, which the rulers of the line of Rurik contracted in the
eleventh century with countries as far away as France, Germany,
Scandinavia and England. There were also commercial bonds
linking the large urban centres of Kiev and Novgorod to the
German countries by the transcontinental route or by the
Baltic. But once the cultural choice had been made and Russia
had adopted the Byzantine form of Christianity, the Russian
church remained adamant, in spite of a few cross-currents in the
course of the eleventh century, insisting on a deliberate and
rigorous isolation from the intellectual centres of western
Latinity.

104, 105 Left, Christ in majesty;
twelfth-century Polish book-
cover. Above, Byzantine sources
transformed into a local style: a
twelfth-century silver chalice from
Novgorod.

109, 110 Far right, the Romanesque abbey church of Ják
in Hungary (thirteenth century). Right, its main porch,
which fuses the current Lombard style, with an ascending gallery,
and the western Romanesque portal with mouldings.

106 The adoration of the Magi, a mid twelfth-century relief
from Pécs cathedral clearly influenced by Lombard statuary.

107, 108 Left, Gertrude, a Polish princess
married to the grand duke of Kiev, presents
her son Jaropolk and his wife Irene to St
Peter; from a late eleventh-century codex.
Above, eleventh-century sacramentary illuminated in the monastery of Tyniec.

In the twelfth century, a new cultural efflorescence occurred in all these countries, borne along, as in the preceding centuries, by social changes which undermined the obsolescent institutions that stood in the way of the consolidation of new economic and political forms.

Contacts with the outside world followed the same routes as before, and Germany and the Empire still occupied the first place. But what is significant is the widening of contacts which now extended as far as the great centres of intellectual revival in western Europe – namely France, Italy, and the Rhineland. Through the flow from the West of manuscripts and artistic designs, of scholars and men of letters, of craftsmen and masons, the Slav and Hungarian élite gained access to that intellectual community which is sometimes called the world of twelfth-century humanism. Conversely, it was sought out at its sources by the Polish, Czech or Hungarian travellers, pilgrims, diplomats or students, whose traces are found on the banks of the

189

111 The thirteenth-century chapel of the royal castle in Esztergom. The appearance of Gothic elements in Hungarian architecture is mainly due to the activity of the Cistercians in eastern Europe.

Tiber, the Rhône, the Seine, the Meuse and the Rhine, and as far as the Holy Land. Even more palpable are the reflections of these contacts in the artistic and literary work which arose in Bohemia in the twelfth century with the *Chronica Boemorum* of Cosmas of Prague, in Hungary with the *Gesta Hungarorum* of the anonymous notary of king Béla, and in Poland with the *Cronicae et gesta ducum sive principum Polonorum* of Gallus Anonymus.

Novelties of all kinds now interested not only the princes and their courts, but also a far wider segment of the nobility than before. The victory of separatist tendencies, which resulted in Poland's falling apart into a series of semi-autonomous duchies from about 1146, promoted a new ferment in social life. The multiplication of centres of political, economic and cultural power meant wider access than before to refinements which had previously been accessible only to those few aristocratic families which had provided the mainstay of the monarchy. We can see the same thing happening in Bohemia, where after the death of Vratislav II in 1002 Moravia became a separate appanage, ruled by the younger sons of the dynasty. Nevertheless Prague and Cracow always retained priority in their two respective countries.

Romanesque Prague, the largest urban centre of the Slav world, with its stout castle of Hradčany, and another at Vyšehrad, its numerous churches and abbeys (over thirty in all), its stone bridge over the Vltava, its great market, its many quarters, and the towers of the merchants' houses, was an important nexus of international commerce where Slavs, Jews and Germans carried on trade. In the realm of art, Bavarian and Italian influences contributed to a remarkable local creativity.

Cracow – the *sedes regni principalis*, or capital, of the ancient Polish monarchy – also formed an urban ensemble comparable to the cities of the West. It numbered at least fifteen Romanesque

112 The medieval quarter of Cracow developed around the market square, with the Gothic and Renaissance cloth hall in the middle. To the right is the tower of the town hall, to the left, St Mary's church.

113, 114 The first Romanesque cathedral of St Wenceslaus in Cracow. Right, the only surviving part, the crypt of St Leonard (1080–1142). Above, an ornamented capital.

churches and was adorned by two important foundations, one supported not by the prince, but by a great nobleman; this was the collegiate church of St Andrew, executed in simple and elegant forms, no less impressive because the scale of its Saxon and Rhineland models was somewhat reduced. The cathedral of St Wenceslaus near the Wawel castle, a princely and episcopal foundation, possessed a double choir, a variant of the designs found in the Rhineland. The catalogues of the cathedral library, preserved for the years 1101 and 1118, show that the collection housed there was an adequate basis for the literary education provided at the cathedral school. Master Vincent, son of a minor knight from the diocese of Cracow, who was promoted to episcopal rank thanks to his intellectual ability, learned the art of rhetoric in this establishment, perfected it in Paris or Orleans, and after his return, composed, towards the end of the twelfth century, a scholarly chronicle of the deeds and exploits of the princes of Poland, a literary work reminiscent of Gervase of Tilbury or John of Salisbury.

115 St Andrew's church in Cracow; view of the two-towered west front (*c.* 1200) which is strongly reminiscent of German westwork.

Another city which rose rapidly in the middle of the twelfth century was Wrocław (or Breslau), the Wratislavia of Latin texts. Owing to the efforts of a local family of the old aristocracy, and of an immigrant prelate from the banks of the Meuse, bishop Gauthier of Malonne, who assumed the functions which elsewhere fell to the prince and built churches, convents, and residences, Wrocław at this time may almost be described as one huge building site. This was, in a sense, the swan-song of the old aristocracy, which was being replaced and was disappearing from the political scene. One of its last artistic monuments in Silesia and Cuiavia was a series of great monumental tympana, after the style of Lombardy and Burgundy, on which the lay founders of churches are represented in conversation with their patron saints.

Nor did eastern Europe escape the great problems troubling the intellectual and spiritual life of the West in the twelfth century; for at least we hear the echoes, diminished in scale, but always perceptible. We do not yet know enough in detail about the choices which had to be made, nor about the adaptation of foreign artistic models to local needs; but it is obvious that assimilation could only be successfully accomplished by reducing the scale of buildings and simplifying design. In this way art and letters, particularly sacred art and pious literature, could be used to implant a global vision of society and the world among the masses of the population. But there is evidence also that projects were undertaken which were not utilitarian in this sense, but intended for an elite. The abbey of the Premonstratensian nuns at Strzelno in central Poland is a fine example of this latter genre. Here we find allegories of spiritual conflict, the rediscovery of certain aspects of nature, cryptic messages in the language of symbolism, all of which are represented in architectural sculpture by masters in stone, who mingle in their artistic vocabulary formulas originating in the different countries of the West.

Another great decorative work, in which the influence of foreign art-forms is evident, is the famous bronze door of

194

118 Henry of Wrocław is presented with a garland by his lady after winning a tournament; from the fourteenth-century Manesse Codex. ▶

116, 117 Left, twelfth-century portal from the church of St Mary Magdalene, Wrocław. Above, detail from the fight between virtues and vices on a Romanesque column in the abbey at Strzelno (*c.* 1200).

119 Christ in majesty with donors, a twelfth-century tympanum carved for the Benedictine abbey in Ołbin under Burgundian stylistic influence.

Gniezno. Similarly, the numerous Cistercian abbeys in Poland, Bohemia and Hungary, built in the Italian, French or German style, like the illuminated manuscripts which were imported or executed on the spot, all revealed the influence of an international ideology, and served to integrate these countries into Latin civilization. But it still remains true that this Romanesque art, although its point of departure was an experience of life which originated in the West, was quite as much an expression of local sensibility as a force which moulded it.

We may conclude this second act in the history of Poland, Czechoslovakia and Hungary in terms of collective psychology, with the judgment that it brought to the ruling classes a realization of their own importance. This sentiment was to prove advantageous in the thirteenth century when the pressure of German civilization and population made it difficult to retain cultural independence, particularly in Bohemia, Silesia, Pomerania and Transylvania. On the whole, the Poles, the Czechs and the Hungarians were more successful in absorbing foreign

120 Christ's entry into Jerusalem; this page from an early thirteenth-century manuscript produced for the Cistercians of Trzebnica shows both stylistic links with the Saxon-Thuringian school and Byzantine elements.

influences than the bordering territories which had to withstand the brunt of the assault, and they enriched their own culture through new impulses acquired during this particularly intensive wave of westernization. Racial identity counted for much in their resistance to German pressure, but in addition they were helped by what we may call the prophylactic role of the Romanesque resurgence of the twelfth century, which strengthened the independent, native foundations of an already fairly advanced civilization and allowed it to grow in a dangerously threatening environment.

The period of the Gothic apogee followed on the Romanesque without any interval or regression. The thirteenth century brought to the surface new social strata, both aristocratic and urban. This in turn widened the composition of the cultured class and shaped it to provide personnel for institutions which, although on the outskirts of Gothic and scholastic Europe, comprised a number of important schools, chanceries, and centres of arts and crafts. In many of these centres the more progressive section of the population spoke the German language, which often distinguished the urban bourgeoisie from the rural aristocracy or the peasants. German was understood in most of the important towns of central Europe: in Bohemia from Prague to Olomouc, in Hungary from Košice to Buda, in Poland from Cracow to Gdańsk. It constituted the bond linking the vast economic and cultural zone stretching from the Vosges and the Alps to the Baltic, the Russian border and the Danube.

Yet the same period saw the appearance of the first literary texts in the Czech and Polish languages which survive to the present day. They date from the end of the twelfth and the thirteenth century. Like the austere Romanesque sculptures of the preceding period, they served to translate religious emotions into artistic forms, in this case poetic and choral: for example, the Czech song *Hospodine, pomilui ny* (Lord, have mercy upon us), and the Polish *Bogurodzica* (Mother of God), both perhaps 197 dating from even earlier times and to be imagined intoned in Romanesque plainsong like the hymns of the Latin and Greek churches. Both of them acquired the status of anthems particularly venerated by the two respective nationalities. And consciousness of the same ethnic identity also inspired the work of historians and hagiographers, as is seen in the *Vita Beatissimi Stanislai* or the *Chronicle of Great Poland*, which even manifests the feeling of belonging to the larger community of the western Slavs, and in the rise of Arpadian historiography with Simon of Kéza in the thirteenth century, and of Czech historiography in the fourteenth century. At the synod of Lęczyca, held in 1285, the Polish clergy proclaimed unanimously that, in order to cultivate and develop the Polish language in the cathedral, monastic and other schools, only those 'who are proficient in this language may be appointed teaching masters, so that they may be in a position to explain the texts to young people in Polish'.

Does the co-existence within the same territory of two different, if not opposing, cultural traditions presage a collision of civilizations, provoking lasting conflicts? It would be a mistake to pose the question in exclusively national terms. Throughout Gothic Europe, and in particular in central Europe, there was pressure towards a uniform style of life which must be called urban. The German influx, unequal though its impact was in different regions, led from the thirteenth century to the co-existence of foreign and indigenous elements in all the countries of eastern Europe. But the countryside where the mass of small landowners and peasants who made up the bulk of the native population lived, and where political power was firmly in the hands of the higher and middle nobility, was largely impervious to foreign influence. It was the towns, particularly the towns of any size, where a bilingualism was encountered in daily business, and where Latin was used in intellectual and to some extent in legal affairs.

In this urban milieu, surrounded sometimes by German villages – for example, in Silesia or in Transylvania – national

121 Head of the Virgin (1477–89) by Veit Stoss; from the high altar of St Mary's church, Cracow.

conflicts remained latent until the moment when the Hussite revolution unleashed them in the first half of the fifteenth century. Otherwise it was much more class than national or ethnic affiliations which accounted for common psychological reactions in the face of certain acute problems. On the other hand, the fact of living together in the same town (in Prague, for example, where there was a German district, the *vicus Teutonicus*, around the church of St Peter from the end of the eleventh century) created opportunities for intellectual exchange and facilitated the interplay of different ways of life, an unfailing source of cultural enrichment. An example of what might happen was the scholar Witelo, born in the thirteenth century in Slavic Silesia of a Thuringian father and a Polish mother, who lived in Italy and France and was the author of a treatise on optics which carried further the ideas of Robert Grosseteste on this subject. Many other examples ranging over several centuries might be quoted, including Veit Stoss of Nuremberg who was active in Cracow during the fifteenth century. They would show how, from the simultaneous contribution of two different ethnic groups, a common civilization – that of the medieval towns and courts – arose with relative harmony in this part of Europe.

199

Cultural progress in Bohemia, Poland and Hungary no longer depended solely on the princes – although all three kingdoms were becoming more centralized during the fourteenth century – nor upon the lay and ecclesiastical aristocracy. Apart from direction from above, an increasingly active part was played by the multi-national urban communities which extolled education and cultivated the arts. Thus in the whole of central Europe art and letters underwent a process of democratization: through the activity of artists working in communities of craftsmen grouped by trade, and through the corporate bodies of scholars, with the universities at their head, artistic themes and intellectual movements were brought to the people in the towns, making them aware of the value of these benefits.

From the second quarter of the thirteenth century brick came into use, and soon revolutionized architecture, allowing countries like central and northern Poland, which are poor in quarry stone, to build both religious and secular monuments more readily. Moreover, brick made it necessary to search for technical solutions different from those demanded by stone, and became one of the basic elements of Gothic art in its northern form, illustrated by surviving buildings extending from Lübeck to Riga, and reaching inland up the valleys of the Elbe, the Oder

122, 123 The fifteenth-century church of St Michael in Cluj, Rumania (left) and the fourteenth-century Great Hall of the guild of St Mary in Riga (right) exemplify the wide geographical extent of late Gothic architecture.

124, 125 Left, Gothic brick architecture of the early fourteenth-century church of St James in Toruń, Poland. Below, late Gothic relief in Reval, representing the arms of the town (1529).

and the Vistula. The countries south of the Carpathians, and to a lesser degree Silesia and Little Poland, were to remain faithful to stone worked in forms inspired by French art and its German imitations; the results are seen in the imposing Gothic ensembles built during the great Czech renaissance under Charles IV, or in Hungary during the Angevin period, and at Cracow and Gniezno under Casimir the Great, the last of the Piast dynasty in Poland.

From the fourteenth century onwards paper imported from France, Italy and Germany, made possible greatly increased activity in the chanceries and counting-houses; from the fifteenth century it was manufactured on the spot, and the result was a great increase in the varieties of written documents. Literary and scholarly activity benefited from it to an equal extent, until with the introduction of printing (Plzeň 1468, Cracow 1473, Buda 1473), it became the mainspring for the whole of intellectual civilization. Painting on wood and sculpture in wood, although known earlier, became widespread only in the fourteenth century; the Czech school of Master Theodoric and the schools of Cracow-Sacz and Pomerania are part of an aesthetic tradition which stretches across the length and breadth of Europe.

In this way centres took shape whose influence extended far beyond their own region. Economic and cultural forces had been generated which could no longer be confined within the framework of a single kingdom. Under the last of the Přemyslids and the Luxembourg dynasty, the political and economic expansion of Bohemia overflowed the boundaries of the ancient Czech territory. The same occurred in Poland under Casimir the Great, whose aspirations for expansion into the Russian East were partly realized at the accession of the Jagiellons by the personal union between Poland and the grand duchy of Lithuania. And Hungary also, under Louis the Great, sought to expand by dynastic union with Poland and Bohemia, a policy revived more than once in the fifteenth century.

126, 127 Left, coronation of the Virgin; detail from the altar of Grudziadz in Poland, c. 1400. Above, St Jerome by Master Theodoric (c. 1360).

This was the time when late Gothic began to emerge clearly as the style of the period, inspired by the desire to form vast unified spaces and masses, examples of which may be found in the great urban churches and town halls. At the same time, the frontier of western art, stabilized in the Romanesque period on the line of the Vistula, the Tisza and the middle reaches of the Danube, shifted eastwards, and in the fifteenth century reached the grand duchy of Lithuania at Wilno (Vilna), its capital, and the Ruthenian lands of the kingdom of Poland in which the ruling classes had for the most part become Catholic after the close of the fourteenth century. This frontier eventually included the whole of Transylvania. Conversely, Russian mural painting of the schools of Volhynia and of Pskov, patronized by Wladislas Jagiello and his son, Casimir IV, penetrated Poland from the east and is met with at the Wawel in Cracow, at Lublin, Sandomir and Wiślica, where substantial works in this style are still extant. The reign of Matthias Corvinus brought Hungary the first breezes of the Florentine Renaissance, which was to reach its peak beyond the Carpathians a generation later.

On the intellectual plane, three universities, the first two of which were to have a great future, began their activities in this part of Europe in the fourteenth century: Prague in 1348, Cracow founded in 1364 and revived in 1397–1400, and Pécs in 1367. Their influence extended over the neighbouring countries, particularly the grand duchy of Lithuania. Founded for the needs of their respective states, they were at the same time international centres of learning – owing to the use of Latin, to recruiting their masters from various countries, and to a brisk exchange of students, manuscripts and ideas. It was from the university of Cracow that the genius of Nicholas Copernicus was to emerge at the end of the fifteenth century.

At the dawn of the modern period, Bohemia, Poland and Hungary were all multi-national political societies with a civilization that was western in character and a place in the international economy. In particular, the Polish-Lithuanian

203

128 St Mary on the Sands (c. 1430) in Wrocław, a late Gothic hall church.

129 The exuberant design of the early sixteenth-century façade of St Anne's church in Wilno marks the final stage in late Gothic architecture.

130 *Agony in the garden*; wall-painting (1415) from the chapel of the Holy Trinity in Lublin. The clearly visible Byzantine influences reached Poland from Russia.

and the Hungarian-Croatian states enjoyed both the advantages and the dangers of their position on the great dividing-line running through the European continent at that time. They served as a bridge between eastern, western and south-eastern Europe, cutting into the spheres of interest of different powers. In the second decade of the sixteenth century, in the Jagiellonian state, this situation was expressed by the establishment of a frontier civilization, western in character but open towards the East. In 1512 the Polish nobility coined the phrase *Rzecz pospolita*, or *res publica*, to denote the Jagiellonian state which belonged as much to central as to eastern Europe, and in 1517 a professor of the university of Cracow borrowed the term *Sarmatia europea* from ancient classical texts for the same purpose.

At the end of the Middle Ages, the centralized Russian state also entered into contact with the West, at least in the degree which seemed necessary in order to enhance its political prestige. For the reconstruction of the Kremlin in Moscow, Russian masters were commissioned; but in 1475, side by side with them, an Italian architect was employed, a skilled engineer who was reasonably flexible in adapting himself to the exigencies of a local tradition many centuries old. In spite of their

131 The town hall in Wrocław (mainly after 1471) exhibits such late Gothic elements as the finely ornamented window bays.

imported technical ingenuity, his cathedral of the Dormition, like the superb palace of the grand princes of Moscow built by two other Italians after 1487, and the ramparts constructed by an Italian team, all embody the principles of old Russian architecture, which, with augmented resources, was still creating its own independent national architectural forms two centuries later than the West.

What conclusions may we draw from this all too brief survey of various aspects of cultural interchange in the countries in the borderlands between eastern and western Europe? Behind the diversity of their political structures, it is possible to discern – as it were across the centuries – a few simple and stable forms which provide the foundations of their civilization. One of these is the region, understood not as a predetermined geographical concept, but as an historical entity in continual evolution, of which, however, certain units form a permanent base. The other is racial identity, drawing on a variety of sources, and maturing in the face of political and cultural challenges. Medieval civilization sought to go beyond nationality and the territorial state, but it was never able to do without their support. Tested in a whirlpool of influences and cross-currents, they contributed to the mutual exchange of values and their continual enrichment in those astonishing medieval societies which, when we approach their problems, we always discover to be nearer to us than we had ever imagined.

132 Anonymous portrait of Nicholas Copernicus (sixteenth century).

This bibliography has been compiled by the editor with the help of information supplied by the contributors. It is necessarily very selective. In particular, no attempt has been made, in a book dealing primarily with the relations between eastern and western Europe, to provide an exhaustive list of the national histories of the countries concerned. The emphasis lies on the area between the Elbe and the Vistula and between the Baltic and the Black Sea, and books dealing with Russian and German history have been excluded, except where they impinge on East-West relations. Some readers may feel that there is little practical advantage, in a series such as this, in referring to works written in the Slavonic languages. In practice, historical writing on eastern Europe in western languages is (with the partial exception of German) notoriously sparse and inadequate, and a bibliography confined to literature in English, German and French would convey little idea either of the sources and secondary material on which contributors have drawn, or of the current state of research. In general, emphasis has been placed on work published since 1945. Since the whole tendency in the post-war period has been to challenge and revise the conventional interpretation of East-West relations, it seems unnecessary, perhaps even undesirable, to refer in detail to literature which current research has superseded, except in cases where it contains indispensable materials.

## NEW PERSPECTIVES ON EAST AND WEST

Some indications of the new trends can be found in G. Barraclough, *History in a Changing World* (Oxford 1955), particularly chs. 3, 4, 12. More fundamental is O. Halecki, *The Limits and Divisions of European History* (London 1951), a vigorous affirmation of the place of the east European peoples in the general pattern of European history. Another historian who has contributed to demolishing old stereotypes is F. Graus, 'Deutsche und Slawische Verfassungsgeschichte', *Historische Zeitschrift* CXCVII (1963) 265–317, and 'Die Entstehung der mittelalterlichen Staaten in Mitteleuropa', *Historica* X (1965) 5–65, where the artificiality of the traditional division between Romano-Germanic and Slav Europe is demonstrated. On the German side perhaps the most important contributions to the revision of traditional views came from H. Ludat, particularly 'Die Slaven und das Mittelalter', *Welt als Geschichte* XII (1952) 69–84, and 'The Oldest Bases of German-Slav Relations', *Eastern Germany. A Handbook* vol. II (Würzburg 1963) 3–32. The shift in historical perspectives was described by K. Bosl, 'Deutsche romantisch-liberale Geschichtsauffassung und "Slavische Legende"', *Bohemia Jahrbuch* V (1964) 12–52, and 'Wandel und Tradition im Geschichtsbild der Deutschen und Tschechen', ibid. VIII (1967) 9–22; cf. also F. Graus and H. Ludat, 'Grundfragen und Schwerpunkte der tschechischen Mediävistik nach 1945', *Studi Medievali* IX (1968) 917–48.

## THE SLAV WORLD

For eastern Europe as a whole S. H. Cross, *Slavic Civilization through the Ages* (Harvard 1948), is still a good short introduction; another is F. Nowak, *Medieval Slavdom and the Rise of Russia* (New York 1930). Less satisfactory, at least for the medieval period, is R. Portal, *The Slavs* (London 1969), but there is a useful survey by H. Kohn, *Die West- und Südslawen* (Frankfurt 1960). F. Dvornik, *The Making of Central and Eastern Europe* (London 1949), is a specialized (and somewhat controversial) study centred on the tenth century, but two further books by the same author, *The Slavs, Their Early History and Civilization* (Boston 1956), and *The Slavs in European History and Civilization* (New Brunswick 1960), provide a

useful, though rather old-fashioned, synthesis of the history of the east European peoples. Another general survey of great merit is O. Halecki, *Borderlands of Western Civilization* (New York 1952). These books tend to concentrate on the area north of the Danube; for the south, or Balkan, Slavs there is a useful history by G. Stadtmüller, *Geschichte Südosteuropas* (Munich 1950), which may be supplemented by T. Stoianovich, *A Study in Balkan Civilization* (New York 1967), a work of a very different type which seeks to analyse change and continuity in Balkan societies from prehistoric to modern times.

On the origins of Slavonic Europe and on Slavonic civilization up to the middle of the thirteenth century, the best source of reference is the great lexicon of Slav antiquity, *Słownik Starożytności Słowiańskich* (*Lexicon antiquitatum Slavicarum*) (Wrocław 1961–, 3 vols. published to date), produced by the Polish Academy of Sciences. It should be supplemented by the standard dictionary of Old Slavonic, *Slovník jazyka staroslověnského* (*Lexicon linguae palaeoslovenicae*), in course of publication by the Czechoslovak Academy of Sciences in Prague since 1959, the *Prolegomena* to which contains a short introduction to the problems and a list of surviving early Slavic works. For those unable to read Polish or Czech, there is a shorter book by J. Filip, *Enzyklopädisches Handbuch zur Ur- und Frühgeschichte Europas* (vol. I, Prague 1966), and L. Niederle, *Manuel de l'antiquité slave* (2 vols.), Paris 1923–26), though the latter has now become outdated in parts as a result of recent archaeological research. J. Eisner, *Rukovět Slovanské archeologie* (Prague 1966), which takes account of new archaeological discoveries, unfortunately remains incomplete owing to the author's death. A useful short survey of recent Russian archaeological research is provided by A. L. Mongait, *Archaeology in the U.S.S.R.* (London 1961). Two other valuable studies are C. Parrott, 'Great Moravia in the Light of Recent Excavations', *Oxford Slavonic Papers* XII (1965) 1–20, and V. Georgiev, 'The Genesis of the Balkan Peoples', *Slavonic and East European Review* XLIV (1966) 285–97, while two books which deal with the period of settlement are *Siedlung und Verfassung der Slawen zwischen Elbe, Saale und Oder*, ed. H. Ludat (Giessen 1960), and *Siedlung und*

*Verfassung Böhmens in der Frühzeit*, ed. F. Graus and H. Ludat (Wiesbaden 1967).

## NATIONAL HISTORIES

Most national histories deal at greater or lesser length with political, diplomatic and cultural relations. The following is a selection of those which may be found useful. For Poland, the most up-to-date work in English is the *History of Poland* by A. Gieysztor, S. Kieniewicz and others, published in Warsaw in 1968. *The Cambridge History of Poland* (vol. I, Cambridge 1950) is uneven, and O. Halecki, *A History of Poland* (1st French ed., Paris 1933; revised ed., London 1961), is slight and rather dated. In German there is a short history by G. Rhode, *Kleine Geschichte Polens* (Darmstadt 1965), and F. Seibt has dealt with *Polen von der Jahrtausendwende bis 1444* in the *Handbuch der europäischen Geschichte*, ed. T. Schieder (vol. II, Stuttgart 1969). An important work in Polish is J. Bardach, *Historia państwa i prawa Polski* (History of the Polish state and law) (vol. I, 2nd ed., Warsaw 1964).

For Bohemia and the Czech lands the classic work is V. Novotný, *České dějiny* (vol. I, pts. 1 and 2, Prague 1912–13), with full documentation. Among modern works F. Kavka, *Přirucka k dejinam Československa do roku 1648* (Prague 1963), a handbook of Czech history to 1648, and Z. Fiala's book on Bohemia under the Přemyslids, *Přemyslovské Čechy* (Prague 1965), may be singled out, and in German the contribution by K. Richter 'Die böhmischen Länder im Früh- und Hochmittelalter', from the sixth century to 1306, with a continuation by F. Seibt from 1306 to 1407, in K. Bosl, *Handbuch der Geschichte der böhmischen Länder* (vol. I, Stuttgart 1967). English-speaking readers must make do with R. W. Seton-Watson, *A History of the Czechs and Slovaks* (London 1943), or S. H. Thomson, *Czechoslovakia in European History* (Princeton 1943).

Works on other east European countries include B. Hóman, *Geschichte des ungarischen Mittelalters* (2 vols., Berlin 1940–43); M. Hellmann, *Das Lettenland im Mittelalter* (Cologne 1954), and *Grundzüge der Geschichte Litauens* (Darmstadt 1966); S. Guldescu, *History of Medieval Croatia* (The Hague 1964); and C. Jireček, *La civilisation serbe au moyen âge* (Paris 1920), a partial translation of his *Staat und Gesellschaft im mittelalterlichen Serbien* (2 vols., Vienna 1912–14).

## POLITICAL RELATIONS

Emphasis (perhaps undue emphasis) has tended to fall on the relations between Germany and its eastern neighbours. Short accounts in English of the course of German eastern expansion will be found in J. W. Thompson, *Feudal Germany* (Chicago 1928) chs. 12–14, G. Barraclough, *The Origins of Modern Germany* (Oxford 1946) ch. 10, and F. L. Carsten, *The Origin of Prussia* (Oxford 1954) chs. 1–5, and there is a recent attempt by H. Schreiber, *Teuton and Slav* (London 1965), to tread a middle line, and to moderate the excess of earlier German historiography. All these tend to be a little old-fashioned, and need reviewing in the light of H. Ludat, 'Die deutsch-polnischen Beziehungen im Licht ihrer geschichtlichen Voraussetzungen', *Nachrichten der Giessener Hochschulgesellschaft* XXVI (1957) 171–

96, and G. Labuda, 'A Historiographic Analysis of the German *Drang nach Osten*', *Polish Western Affairs* V (1964) 221–65, a review of the changing attitudes of historians on both the German and the Polish sides. There is a recent German reassessment by W. Schlesinger, 'Die geschichtliche Stellung der mittelalterlichen deutschen Ostbewegung', *Historische Zeitschrift* CLXXXIII (1957) 517–42.

Writing on more specialized aspects includes K. Bosl, 'Das Grossmährische Reich in der politischen Welt des 9. Jahrhunderts', *Sitzungsberichte der bayerischen Akademie der Wissenschaften, phil.-hist. Klasse* (Munich 1966) Heft 7; F. Graus, 'Origines de l'état et de la noblesse en Moravie et en Bohême', *Revue des études slaves* XXXIX (1961); T. Manteuffel, 'L'état de Miesco Ier et les relations internationales au Xe siècle', *Revue historique* CCXXVIII (1962); A. Gieysztor, 'Christiana respublica et la politique orientale de l'Empire', in *Renovatio Imperii* (Faenza 1963); H. Ludat, 'The medieval Empire and the early Piast state', *Historical Studies* VI (London 1966) 1–21; F. Dvornik, 'The first wave of the *Drang nach Osten*', *Cambridge Historical Journal* VII (1943) 129–45; M. Hellmann, 'Uber die Grundlagen und die Entstehung des Ordensstaates in Preussen', *Nachrichten der Giessener Hochschulgesellschaft* XXXI (1962) 108–26. G. Stökl, *Osteuropa und die Deutschen* (Oldenburg and Hamburg 1967), is an attempt at a modern synthesis.

If historians for the most part have concentrated on the western, particularly the German impact on eastern Europe, it is important also not to neglect contacts with other areas, particularly Byzantium and Russia. The position of the peoples of the 'borderlands', balanced between East and West, was briefly surveyed by F. Dvornik, 'Western and Eastern Traditions in Central Europe', *Review of Politics* IX (1947) 463–81, and there is a general conspectus in a composite work, *Russland, Europa und der deutsche Osten* (ed. Krusius and others), published at Munich in 1960. 'The Historical Limits of the Question of Russia and the West' were discussed by M. Szeftel, *Slavic Review* XXIII (1964) 20–27, and A. V. Florovsky, *Čechi i vostočnye Slavjane* (vol. I, Prague 1935), provides an outline of Russo-Czech relations in the Middle Ages and later. For early Russian relations with the West (commercial relations will be treated separately below) G. Stökl, 'Russland und Europa vor Peter dem Grossen', *Historische Zeitschrift* CLXXXIV (1957) 531–54, is a useful short survey. Byzantine influence was mainly expressed through the church, and this will be considered in the following section, but there are also two works of wider bearing: E. E. Lipšic, *Byzanz und die Slaven* (Weimar 1951), and a parallel work for Hungary, G. Moravcsik, *Bizánc és magyarság* (Budapest 1953).

## THE IMPACT OF CHRISTIANITY

D. Obolensky has written an excellent short account of the work of 'Sts. Cyril and Methodius, Apostles of the Slavs', *St. Vladimir's Seminary Quarterly* VII (1963) 1–10. For 'The Beginning of Christianisation in Great Moravia', see an article under this title by Z. R. Dittrich, *Slavonic and East European Review* XXXIX (1960) 164–73, and K. Bosl, 'Probleme der Missionierung des böhmisch-mährischen Herrschaftsraumes', in *Siedlung und Verfassung Böhmens in der Frühzeit*, ed. F. Graus and H. Ludat (Wiesbaden 1967)

104–32. G. Moravcsik has written on 'Byzantine Christianity and the Magyars in the Period of their Migration', *American Slavonic and East European Review* v (1948) 29–45, and A. Gieysztor on 'Les paliers de la pénétration du Christianisme en Pologne au $X^e$ er $XI^e$ siècles', *Studi in onore di Amintore Fanfani* (vol. I, Milan 1962) 327–67. P. Kehr, 'Das Erzbistum Magdeburg und die christliche Kirche in Polen', *Abhandlungen der Berliner Akademie der Wissenschaften, phil.-hist. Klasse*, no. 1 (1920), is an important study of the abortive attempt by the German emperors to erect Magdeburg into a metropolitan see for the entire East.

More general works on the Christian missions are F. Dvornik, *Les Slaves, Byzance et Rome au IXe siècle* (Paris 1926); G. Stökl, 'Geschichte der Slavenmission', in *Die Kirche in ihrer Geschichte*, ed. K. D. Schmidt and E. Wolf (vol. II, Göttingen 1963); and B. Stasiewski, 'Zur Geschichte der Christianisierung Ostmitteleuropas', in *Leistung und Schicksal*, ed. E. G. Schulz (Cologne 1967). For the development of the church in Poland and the relations of church and state until the beginning of the fourteenth century S. Krakowski, *Kościół i państwo polskie do początków XIV wieku* (Warsaw 1950), is important, and G. Székely, 'Gemeinsame Züge der ungarischen und polnischen Kirchengeschichte des XI. Jahrhunderts', *Annales Universitatis Scientiarum Budapestensis, Sectio Historica* IV (1962) 55–80, compares the development of the Hungarian and Polish churches in the eleventh century. The impact of western monasticism is described by P. David, *Les Bénédictins et l'ordre de Cluny dans la Pologne médiévale* (Paris 1939), and T. Manteuffel, *Cystersi w Polsce* (Warsaw 1955), the latter on the Cistercians. K. Gorski, *Od religijności do mystiki, zarys dziejów życia wewnetrznego w Polsce* (Lublin 1962), traces the rise of mysticism and its impact on lay society in the fourteenth century.

The Hussite movement is a major topic with a large and growing literature, and only a few outstanding works can be mentioned here. These include, in English, J. Macek, *The Hussite Movement in Bohemia* (Prague 1958), and H. Kaminsky, *A History of the Hussite Revolution* (Berkeley 1967); in Czech, R. Kalivoda, *Husitská ideologie* (Prague 1961); and in German, the works of F. Seibt, *Hussitica. Zur Struktur einer Revolution* (Cologne 1965), and 'Die hussitische Revolution und die europäische Gesellschaft', *Cultus Pacis*, ed. V. Vaneček (Prague 1966) 21–33.

## TRADE AND ECONOMIC RELATIONS

The literature on East-West trade, mainly monographs on single towns or regions, is very considerable, but attempts at synthesis are few. M. Małowist, 'The Problem of the Inequality of Economic Development in the Later Middle Ages', *Economic History Review* (2nd ser.) XIX (1966) 15–28, is a useful introduction which assesses the relative importance of long-distance and local trade in the economic development of the east European states, while A. Gieysztor outlines 'Les structures économiques en pays slaves à l'aube du moyen âge jusqu'au $XI^e$ siècle et l'échange monétaire' in *Settimane di Studio del Centro Italiano di Studi Sull' alto medioevo* IX (Spoleto 1961).

General accounts of trade in northern Europe will be found in M. M. Postan, 'The Trade of Medieval Europe: the North', *Cambridge Economic History* (vol. II, Cambridge 1952); A. Lewis, *The Northern Seas. Shipping and Commerce in Northern Europe, A.D. 300–1100* (Princeton 1958); and P. Klettler, *Nordwesteuropas Verkehr, Handel und Gewerbe im frühen Mittelalter* (Vienna 1924), while the trade routes linking East and West are discussed by A. Bugge, 'Die nordeuropäischen Verkehrswege im früheren Mittelalter', *Vierteljahrschrift für Sozial- und Wirtschaftsgeschichte* IV (1906); T. Wasowicz, 'Le réseau routier de la Pologne du $IX^e$ au $XIII^e$ siècle', *Le Moyen Age* LXVIII (1962) 379–94; and T. Lewicki, 'Certaines routes commerciales de la Hongrie du haut Moyen Age', *Slavia Antiqua* XIV (1967). For the slave trade, so important in the early period, the best account is in C. Verlinden, *L'esclavage dans l'Europe médiévale* I (Bruges 1955); the classic account of the Scandinavian timber trade is A. Bugge, *Den Norske Traelasthandels Historie* I (Skien 1925).

The trade links between the lands of central Europe and the eastern Mediterranean (Byzantium, the Black Sea and the Moslem world) are discussed by T. Lewicki, 'Il commercio arabo con la Russia e con i paesi slavi d'occidente nei secoli IX–XI', *Annali dell' Istituto Universitario Orientali di Napoli* VIII (1959); S. Kutrzeba, 'Handel Polski ze Wschodem w wiekach średnich' (Poland's trade with the Orient in the Middle Ages), *Przegląd Polski*, nos. 148–50 (Cracow 1903); and I. Dujcev, 'Rapporti economici fra Bisanzio e gli Slavi', *Bolletino dell' Istituto Storico Italiano per il Medioevo* LXXVI (1964). On trade between Russia and the West, cf. L. K. Goetz, *Deutsch-Russische Handelsgeschichte des Mittelalters* (Lübeck 1922); P. Johansen, *Der hansische Russlandhandel, insbesondere nach Novgorod* (Cologne 1962); B. Widera, 'Wirtschaftliche Beziehungen zwischen Deutschland und der Kiever Rus', *Zeitschrift für Geschichtswissenschaft* 1 (1954); A. L. Khoroshkievich, *Torgovlia Velikovo Novgoroda s Pribaltikoi i Zapadnoi Eüropoi v. XIV–XV vv* (The Trade of Great Novgorod with the Baltic Countries and Western Europe in the XIV and XV centuries) (Moscow 1963).

For trade between Poland, Germany and Flanders, see H. Ammann, 'Wirtschaftsbeziehungen zwischen Oberdeutschland und Polen', *Ergon* III (1962); M. Małowist, 'Le développement des rapports économiques entre la Flandre, la Pologne et les pays imitrophes du XIII$^e$ au XV$^e$ siècle', *Revue belge de philologie et d'histoire* x (1931); C. Warnke, *Die Anfänge des Fernhandels in Polen, 900–1025* (Würzburg 1964); N. W. Posthumus, *De Oostersche Handel te Amsterdam* (Leiden 1953); and M. P. Lesnikov, 'Niderlands i Vostochnaya Baltika', *Izvestia Akademii Nauk U.S.S.R.* (1951). Lesnikov has also written on 'Lübeck als Handelsplatz für Osteuropa Waren im 15. Jahrhundert', *Hansische Studien* (Berlin 1961), and on the important fur trade, 'Der hansische Pelzhandel zu Beginn des 15. Jahrhunderts' (ibid.). Finally, E. E. Power and M. M. Postan, *Studies in English Trade in the Fifteenth Century* (London 1933), is still one of the best accounts of the salt trade and of the factors affecting commercial relations between the Baltic and the West in this period.

The trading connections between southern Germany

(Nuremberg, Regensburg) and Bohemia (Prague), extending east to southern Poland (Cracow), Transylvania and Moldavia, are discussed by K. Bosl, 'Wirtschaftlichpolitische Beziehungen der Residenz- und Fernhandelsstadt Regensburg zum slavischen Osten', *Beiträge zur Südosteuropa-Forschung* (Munich 1966) 316–25; F. Graus, 'Die Handelsbeziehungen Böhmens zu Deutschland und Österreich im 14. und zu Beginn des 15. Jahrhunderts', *Historica* II (1960); F. Graus, *Český obchod se suknem ve 14. a počátkem 15. stoleti* (Prague 1950), a study of the Czech cloth trade; S. Kutrzeba, *Handel Krakowa w wiekach średnich* (Cracow 1903); and L. Charewiczowa, *Handel średniowiecznego Lwowa* (Lvov 1925), for the trade of medieval Cracow and Lvov respectively. This brief and selective list may be completed by two older books, T. Mayer, *Der auswärtige Handel des Herzogtums Österreich im Mittelalter* (Innsbruck 1909), for Austria, and J. Nistor, *Die auswärtigen Handelsbeziehungen der Moldau im XIV., XV. und XVI. Jahrhundert* (Gotha 1911), for Moldavia. Finally, A. Gieysztor has surveyed 'Local Markets and Foreign Exchanges in Central and Eastern Europe before 1200' in *Ergon* V (1966).

CULTURAL CONTACTS AND DEVELOPMENTS

A useful collection of studies on various aspects of cultural history will be found in the proceedings of the eleventh congress of Polish historians, published under the title *Histoire de la culture médiévale en Pologne* (Warsaw 1963). For Russia the two volumes of *Istoriya Kultury drevney Rusi* (Moscow 1948–51) are a key work for the period up to the thirteenth century, and there is a brief guide by D. S. Likhatchev, *Kultura russkogo naroda X–XVII vv.* (Moscow 1961). B. D. Grekov, *The Culture of Kiev Rus* (Moscow 1949), is a well-known introduction, with a rather nationalistic tinge, and D. Obolensky, 'Russia's Byzantine Heritage', *Oxford Slavonic Papers* I (1950) 37–63, is an assessment of the part played by Byzantine influences in the development of Russian civilization. F. Graus, *Dějiny venkovského lidu v Čechách v době predhusitské* I (Prague 1953), though dealing more particularly with the peasantry, is really a social history of medieval Bohemia, and there is an older work by J. Lippert, *Socialgeschichte Böhmens in vorhussitischer Zeit* (2 vols., Prague 1896–98). The process of social diversification and stratification is discussed by H. Łowmiański, 'La génèse des états slaves et ses bases sociales et économiques', in *Collected Papers on Polish History at the Tenth International Congress of Historical Sciences* (Warsaw 1955); F. Graus, 'Adel, Land und Herrscher in Böhmen vom 10. bis 13. Jahrhundert', *Nachrichten der Giessener Hochschulgesellschaft* XXXV (1966) 131–53; and G. Rhode, 'Stände und Königtum in Polen-Litauen und Böhmen-Mähren', *Jahrbücher für Geschichte Osteuropas* XII (1964) 221–46, and among a growing literature on the rise of towns reference may be made to A. Gieysztor, 'Aux origines de la ville slave', *Cahiers Bruxellois* XII (1967); H. Ludat, 'Vorstufen und Entstehung des Städtwesens in Osteuropa', *Osteuropa und der deutsche Osten*, 3rd ser., no. 4 (1955); and

J. M. Pesez, 'Archéologie Slave: Villes et Campagne', *Annales* XXII (1967).

L. Mezey, *Irodalmi anyanyelvüségünk kezdetei az Árpádkor végén* (Budapest 1955), discusses the beginnings of vernacular literature in Hungary, and the beginnings of Polish and Czech literature, respectively, are briefly surveyed in J. Krzyżanowski, *Historia literatury polskiej* (Warsaw 1964) 9–85, and J. Hřabak (and others), *Dějiny české literatury* (vol. I, Prague 1959). The classic edition of Serbian epic poetry is V. S. Karadžić, *Srpske narodne pjesme* (Belgrade 1953), which may be supplemented by A. B. Lord, *Serbocroatian Heroic Songs* (Harvard 1954). M. Murko, *Geschichte der älteren südslawischen Litteraturen* (Leipzig 1908), is a standard work, while the contributions by V. M. Zirmunsky and J. G. Bogatyrev to the proceedings of the Fourth International Congress of Slavists (Moscow 1958) and the relevant articles in *Osnovnye problemy eposa vostočnyh Slavjan* (Moscow 1958) are important for the comparative history of the Slav epic. There is also an important article by D. A. Likbachev on 'The Type and Character of the Byzantine Influence on Old Russian Literature' in *Oxford Slavonic Papers* XIII (1967) 14–32.

On the development of art in Poland, the standard work is F. Kopera, *Średniowieczne Malarstwo w Polsce* (Cracow 1925), and there are more recent surveys by M. Walicki, *Malarstwa Polskie* (Warsaw 1961), and T. Dobrowolski and W. Tatarkiewicz, *Historia Sztuki Polskiej* (vol. I, Cracow 1962). For medieval architecture in Poland, see J. Zachwatowicz, *Architektura Polska* (Warsaw 1956), and Z. Swiechowski, *Budownictwo romańskie w Polsce* (Wrocław-Warzawa-Krakow 1963), while, for more specialized topics in art history, there is Z. Ameisenowa, *Rękopisy i Pierwodruki Illuminowane Biblioteki Jagiellońskiej* (Wrocław-Krakow 1958), on illustrated manuscripts; P. Skubiszewski, *Czara Włocławska* (Poznań 1965), on the minor arts; and T. Dobrowolski, *Sztuka Krakowa* (Cracow 1950), on the arts in Cracow. For Hungary, reference may be made to A. Hekler, *Ungarische Kunstgeschichte* (Berlin 1937), and T. Gerevich, *Romanesque monuments of Hungary* (Budapest 1938). The standard work on Gothic painting in Bohemia is A. Matejcek, *Gotische Malerei in Böhmen* (Prague 1940), and *Dějepis výtvarných umění v československu* (Prague 1933), is a useful symposium on Czech art. For the Great Moravian empire, there is an informative catalogue of an exhibition arranged by the Römisch-Germanisches Zentralmuseum, *Grossmähren. Slawenreich zwischen Byzantinern und Franken* (Mainz 1966). K. Benda and K. Neubert have written on *Ornament and Jewellery: archaeological finds from Eastern Europe*, trans. L. Urwin (Prague 1967). For Russia, in addition to G. H. Hamilton, *The Art and Architecture of Russia* (London 1954), there is an elaborate history of medieval Russian art, translated from the Russian, *Geschichte der russichen Kunst*, ed. I. E. Grabar, W. N. Lazarev and W. S. Kemenov (3 vols., Dresden 1957–59). W. Weidlé discusses 'Some Common Traits in Early Russian and Western Arts' in *Oxford Slavonic Papers* IV (1953) 17–37.

# SOURCES OF ILLUSTRATIONS

# INDEX

*Page references to illustrations are given in italics*

Adalbert, St, bishop of Prague 98–9; *99*, *126*
Adalbert, archbishop of Magdeburg 94
Adamklissi victory monument *20*
Adolph of Holstein 145
Agnes of Bohemia, St 115
Akerman 133
Albrecht of Habsburg 80
Albrecht of Hohenzollern 72
Alfeld, church near *101*
Andrew III of Hungary 74
Angevin line of Hungary 74, 77–8
Antwerp 151
archaeology, evidence of 18–19, 31–5, 37, 47, 136, 140, 179, 183; *19*, *33*, *34*, *39*, *47*, *48*, *89*, *136–9*, *147*, *177*, *181*
architecture 12, 90, 111, 185, 192, 194, 196, 200–6 *passim*; *91*, *95*, *101*, *104*, *105*, *111*, *119*, *145*, *163*, *164*, *185*, *188*, *190–3*, *195*, *200*, *201*, *204*, *205*
Arnulf 41
Arpad dynasty 10, 58, 74, 93
Ascherich, archbishop 99
Augsburg 129, 152
Augustinian Order 104, 112
Austria 27, 44, 65, 73, 74, 77, 78, 157
Avars 45, 47, 94

Babenberg dynasty 64, 73
Baltic region 99, 110, 130, 145, 146–66 *passim*, 182, 184, 187
Basel, Council of 79–80, 123
*Bauernlegen* 172–3
Bavaria 157, 184, 185, 191
beeswax, trade in 155, 156
Beghard movement 116
Beguine movement 115–16
Béla IV of Hungary 73
Belgium 124
Benedictine Order 95–101 *passim*, 103
Berengar of Tours 120
Bergen 149
Bernard of Clairvaux, St 65, 106
Birka, finds *136*, *138*
Biscay salt production 163–4
Black Death 149
Black Sea 130, 132
*Boguodzica* 197–8

Bohemia 12, 21, 26ff, 35–40 *passim*, 44, 49, 50, 54, 56–7, 65ff, 73, 74, 77–82 *passim*, 93–8 *passim*, 101, 102, 106, 113, 116, 117, 121, 128–9, 143, 149, 175, 176, 178, 180–6 *passim*, 190–1, 196, 197, 200, 202; *181*; *see also* Hus; Prague
'Bohemian Brethren', community of 123
Boleslav I Chrobry 52, 54, 55, 93, 182; *126*
Boleslav II 100
Boniface, St 86; *88*
*Book of Maccabees 49*
Bordeaux 162
Borna 49
Borucin, grave find *181*
Boso, bishop of Merseburg 97
Brandenburg 65, 67, 143
Bratislava 129
Bremen, archbishopric of 94
Breslau 107, 130, 194; St Mary Magdalene *195*; St Mary on the Sands *204*; Town Hall *205*
'Brethren of the Free Spirit' 115
Brevnov monastery 98
brewing 162
Brno 129
Bruges 148, 151, 152, 164
Bruno, bishop of Olmütz 107
Bug, R. 44
Bulgaria and Bulgars 10, 58, 78, 84, 138, 184
Byzantium 10, 21, 41, 43, 51, 58, 83–5, 87, 95, 130, 135, 136, 139, 175, 176, 184; *137*, *187*, *196*, *204*; *see also* Greek Orthodox religion

Caffa 132–3
Calixtines 122
canon law 103
Carinthia 49, 73
Carniola 73
Carthusian Order 112, 113
Casimir the Great 13, 62, 69, 110, 112, 131, 201, 202; *70*
Casimir IV 203; *81*
Castlenau-de-Guers, sarcophagus *85*
castles *32*, *63*
celibacy 103
Česke Budejovice, grave find *181*
Charlemagne 43, 47, 56, 83, 86

Charles IV (the Great) of Bohemia 13, 62, 75, 110, 111, 112, 118, 201; *76*
Charles Robert, king of Hungary 74, 78
Chelčický, Peter 123
Cherson 132
China 139
Christianity *see* religion
*Chronica Boemorum* 190
*Chronicle of Great Poland* 199
*Chronicon Aulae Regiae* 75
Cistercian Order 12, 106, 113, 196; *104, 190*
cloth trade 164–6; *164, 165*
Cluj, St Michael's *200*
Cluniac Order 13, 97, 100
coinage 129, 136, 140; *33, 53, 137, 138*
Cologne 144, 166, 180
Comenius, J. A. 22
commerce *see* trade
Conrad of Masovia 70, 110; *71*
Constance, Council of 79, 120, 121
Copernicus, Nicholas 203; *206*
Cosmas of Prague 35, 190
Cracow 107, 124, 130, 152, 191–2, 199, 201, 203; *191*; cathedral, tombs in *70, 81*; St Andrew's *192*; *193*; St Mary's *199*; St Wenceslaus' *192*; *192*
Croats 49, 57
*Cronicae et gesta ducum sive principum Polonorum* 190
Cuiavia 194
Cunegonde, abbess, Passionary of *76*
Cyril, St 10, 40, 58, 87, 184; *87*
Czechs 50, 66, 74, 79, 182, 184, 196, 197, 198, 202

'Dagome iudex' 51
Dalmatia 49, 78, 184, 185
Danube, R. 45, 54, 130, 132
Danzig *see* Gdańsk
*De Ecclesia* (Hus) 120
Denmark 111
Derwan 46
*Devotio Moderna* 118
Dnieper, R. 44
Dniester, R. 132
Dobrovský, Josef 25
Dominican Order 114–15
*Drang nach Osten* 7, 42, 43, 60–73 *passim*, 141ff; *142, 145*
Dražic, bishop John 112; *108*
Dušan, Stefan 57, 78

Eckhart, Meister 115
Eichstätt monastery, inventory *173*
Einhard 31
Elbe, R. 11, 46, 129, 144, 174, 184
Elisabeth of Poland 78
England 12, 124, 135, 151, 156, 157, 158, 161, 162, 165–6, 170
episcopacy 50, 56, 91, 94, 95, 98ff

Erzgebirge 66
Esztergom, cathedral of St Adalbert 185; *185*; royal castle *190*

feudal system 141, 167ff
fishing 164, 166
Flagellants 115
Flanders 12, 161, 162, 164–5, 166, 169
forests, reduction of 157; *see also* timber trade
France 12, 58, 83, 128, 157, 158, 161–2, 170, 187, 189
Franciscan Order 114–15
Franconia 169
Franks, influence of 46, 85–7; artefacts *39, 41*
Frederick III 82
Frisia 135, 161
Fulda Sacramentary *88*
fur trade 154–5

Galicia 69
'Gallus Anonymus' 35
Gästrikland, reliquary from *137*
Gaudentius, archbishop 99
Gauthier of Malonne, bishop 194
Gdańsk 72, 146, 148, 152, 159, 162, 164, 165, 166
Geislingen *164*
Genoa 132–3
George of Poděbrad (king of Bohemia) 82, 124; *81*
*Germania* (Tacitus) 17, 22
Germanicus 6
Germany: eastward movement *see Drang nach Osten*; feudalism 170–4; founding of independent kingdom 89; imperial policy towards east 52–6; language 197; peoples, concept of from 18th cent. 22–5; trading 144–66 *passim*; 'unity' 30, 36–7
Gertrude, princess *188*
*Gesindezwang* 172
*Gespräch des Ackermanns mit dem Tod* 117
*Gesta Hungarorum* 190
Gniezno 51, 52, 94, 99, 107, 196, 201; cathedral *99, 126*
Golden Bull of Charles IV *113*
Gorze monastery 97
Gothic culture 197ff
Gotland, hoards *137, 139*
Gradual of Malá Strana *118*
grain trade 133, 160–3, 166, 172, 174; *163*
Gran, archbishopric of 94, 95
Great Moravian empire 35, 38, 47, 49; *34, 47*
Greek Orthodox religion 10, 26, 27, 51, 83–5, 87, 94, 95, 187
Grimm, Jacob and Wilhelm 23
Groote, Gert 118
Grudziadz, altar *202*
Güdingen, grave find *39*

Haakon Hakonsen, king 161

Haithabu, coin hoard *138*
Halecki, Oskar 13, 14
Hamburg 147, 151, 152, 162, 163
Hanseatic League 147–66 *passim*
Hausbuch Master *152*
Hazars 138–9
Hegel, Friedrich 23
Hellweg route 144
Henry I of Germany 56
Henry II of Germany 11, 93–4, 99; *93*
Henry IV, emperor 100
Henry of Breslau *194*
Henry the Lion, duke of Saxony 67
Herder, Johann Gottfried 22, 25, 28
Hermann of Salza 70–1
Hirsch, Theodore 159
Holy Roman Empire 43, 47, 52, 54, 56, 66–7, 77; *84, 93*
*Hospodine, pomilui ny* 197–8
Hungary 12, 13, 40, 44, 46, 51, 57, 58, 62, 73–8 *passim*, 80, 93, 100, 102, 106, 107, 109, 113, 116, 123, 128, 130, 178, 180ff, 190, 196, 197, 200–5 *passim*
Hus, Jan, and Hussites 73, 79, 80, 119–24, 199; *118, 119*

Ibrahim ibn Jaqub 31
*Ideen zur Philosophie der Geschichte der Menschheit* (Herder) 22
Illuminated books and MSS. 196; *49, 53, 75, 76, 80, 81, 87, 88, 93, 96, 97, 108, 113, 116, 164, 187, 194, 196*
Ilvesheim grave finds *19*
'Innocent Children' centre 119
Investiture contest 102
Ireland 86
Italy 12, 58, 78, 83, 84, 97, 112, 128, 133, 152, 185, 189, 191
Ivan the Terrible 170

Jacobellus of Mies 121, 122
Jagiellon dynasty 71–2, 78
Ják abbey church *189*
Jena Codex *80*
Jenstein, John, archbishop of Prague 112
Jihtnovo silver mines 129
Joan of Arc 124
Johannes of Saaz, work by *117*
John of Bohemia 69
John Hunyadi, king of Hungary 82
John of Luxembourg 75
*Junkers* 170–4
Jutland peninsula 147, 150

Kalivoda 122
Kiev 33, 38, 39, 43, 57, 60, 94, 100, 131–2, 138, 180, 187; *188*; artefact *131*; Hagia Sophia *59*
Kilia 133
Koczowski, J. 101

Kolin, grave find *177*
Königinhof and Grünberg MSS. 28
Königsaal abbey 133
Korvey 97
Kossovo, battle of 78
Kravář, Pavel 124
Kremsier, canon Milič 118
Kutna Hora silver mines 129

Latvia 146
Lausitz 65, 77, 93
lay devotion 115ff
Lech, battle of 51
Lęczyca, synod of 198; castle reconstruction *32*
Lelewel, Joachym 27, 28
Levantine trade 125ff, 135
Liège 12, 99, 166, 180
Lipany, battle of 80
Lithuania 71, 72, 176, 202, 203
Liutizi 11, 68, 94
Livonia 146
Lombardy style 194; *185, 188*
London 149, 154
Louis the German 89
Louis the Great of Hungary 13, 77, 78, 110, 112, 202; *79*
Low Countries 12, 151, 154, 156, 161, 162, 164–5; *165*
Lübeck 138, 145–6, 147, 151, 152; *163*
Lublin, Holy Trinity chapel *204*
Ludat, H. 94
Lund, archbishopric of 94
Lüneburg salt production 163
Lusatians 64
Luther, Martin 124; *118*
Lwow 130, 152

Magdeburg 55, 94, 95, 104, 144
Magyars 49, 51, 54, 56, 89, 183; *49*
Main, R. 45, 46
Mainz, archbishopric of 50
*Malogranatum* (devotional book) 113; *113*
Manesse Codex *194*
March valley 47; crucifix from *89*
Marches, imperial system of 56
Marchfeld, battle of 21, 74
Marcus Aurelius, Column of *18*
Margaret of Hungary, St 115
Marienburg castle *63*
Mariengarten monastery 112
Masovia 70–1
Matthias Corvinus 13, 82, 203; *81*
Matthias of Janov 118
Mecklenburg 65, 143
Mecklenburg-Schwerin/Strelitz dynasty 182
Meissen 54, 56, 65, 92
mendicant Orders 114–15
Methodius, St 10, 40, 58, 87, 88, 184; *87*
Mieszko I 51, 93, 182

Mikulčice palace *47*; rotunda *48*; finds *89*, *177*
mining 129, 130, 152; *152*
missionary activity by Christian Church 40–1,
    55–7, 83–100 *passim*
Moldavia 132, 133
Mongol invasion 61, 73, 109, 176
Monomach, prince Vladimir 60
Moravia 33, 40–1, 47, 58, 66, 87, 88, 89, 107, 113,
    123, 128–9, 175, 178, 179, 184, 191; *see also*
    Great Moravian empire
Morken grave find *39*
Moscow 61, 72, 75; Kremlin 205–6
Murad I 78

Nagyszentmiklós treasure *181*
national feeling in the Church 108–9, 111
nationalism, Bohemian 78ff; *181*
Neisse, R. 107
'Neustämme' 68–9
Niederaltaich 97
Norbert of Xanten 67, 104
Normandy 170
Norway 157–8, 160–1
Notger, bishop 180
Novgorod 148, 164, 187; chalice from *187*
Nuremberg 129, 152, 199; trade book from *165*

Obodrites 36, 46, 64, 68, 182
Obra Nowa coin hoard *33*
Odilo, abbot of Cluny 99
Ołbin abbey, tympanum *195*
Oldcastle, Lord 124
Orders, religious 83–100 *passim*, 104–7, 112–15,
    194, 196
Osek monastery, chapter house *104*
Ostrov monastery 97
Otakar II of Bohemia 21, 62, 73, 74; *75*
Otto I 55, 56, 94; *55*
Otto II *84*
Otto III 52, 54, 57, 93, 98, 99; *55*

Palacký, František 27, 28
Pannonia 47, 49
papacy 51, 83, 86, 100, 102, 110, 123, 143
paper 201–2
parochial system 101–2, 107
Payne, Peter 124
Pécs 203; *188*
Perejaslavl 131
*Philosophy of History* (Hegel) 23
Piast dynasty 10, 52, 58, 69, 93, 178, 183
Picardists 124
*Picture Chronicle* (Hungarian) *53*, *79*
*Ploughman of Bohemia, The 117*
Poland 11, 26, 27, 33, 35, 36, 40, 51–2, 54, 58,
    60, 61–2, 67ff, 74, 78, 93, 98, 100, 101, 102, 106,
    108, 109, 110, 113, 116, 124, 128, 130–1, 146,
    149, 152, 156, 166, 171ff, 180–6 *passim*, 190,
    196ff, 202, 205; coinage *53*

Polotsk 148
Pomerania 65, 143, 196
Poznań 51, 98; cathedral of St Peter 185
Prague 49, 50, 60, 75, 77, 97, 111, 118ff, 129, 191,
    199; Old Town Bridge Tower *111*; St George's
    *95*; St Guy's 185; St Vitus' cathedral *111*; Týn
    church *119*
Prague, Compacts of 80
Prague, Four Articles of 123
Premonstratensian Order 104, 106, 194; *105*
Přemyslid dunasty 50, 58, 74, 93, 98, 178; *75*
Pribina 46
printing 202
Pripet, R. 44
Procop 79, 122
Procopius of Caesarea 18
proprietary churches 101–2; *101*
Prussia 67, 70–1; 110, 143, 146, 166, 170
Prussian Union 72
Pskov 148

race 9, 35, 36, 197, 206
*Radziwill Chronicle* 87
Ranke, Leopold von 7–8, 9, 24–5, 42
Rastislav 87, 89
Raudnitz 112
Regensburg 12, 50, 58, 95, 152, 180
regionalism 206
Reichenau 97
religion 10, 26, 36, 40–1, 50, 51, 54–7, 83–124
    *passim*, 185, 187, 194, 196, 197
Renaissance 13, 78, 124, 203
'Renovatio' 52
Reval 112, 146; town arms *201*
Rhadanites 139; *126*
Rhine and Rhineland 12, 46, 144, 185, 192
Riga 146; Guild Hall *200*
Rokycana, Jan 122
Roman empire 13, 16–18; *18*
Rome 83, 180
Rostock 146
Rothenburg 129
royalty, concepts of 38, 50
Rudolf IV of Habsburg 21, 74, 111; *110*
Rumania 123
Rurik dynasty 187
Russia 10, 24, 26, 27, 128, 131–3, 135, 156, 159–
    60, 170–8 *passim*, 182, 184, 187, 203, 205–6
Ruysbroek, Jan van 115

Saale, R. 46
Sady, church at *91*
Šafařík, Pavel Josef 25
St Emmeram abbey 95, 97
St Gallen 180; MS. from *49*
salt trade 163–4; *163*
Salzburg, archbishopric of 94, 95
Samo 46
San Alessio monastery, Rome 98

*Sarmatia europea* 205
Savernake Forest 157
Saxons 86, 142, 154
Sázava, abbey of 184
Scandinavia 94, 135–40, 151, 154, 157, 158, 160–1, 162, 164, 184; *136*
secular clergy 100–1, 103, 104
Serbs 10, 57, 78, 84
shipbuilding 156, 158; *159*
Sigismund, emperor 78–9, 80, 121
Silesia 65, 69–70, 122, 123, 129–30, 143, 149, 194, 196, 198
silver, Bohemian supplies of 129
Simon of Kéza 199
Skania 147, 164
Slav: culture 175–206 *passim*; mission 95, 97; peoples, differences between 26, 31, 33, 35–6; political institutions 37–40; social order 184ff; 'unity' 30–7 *passim*; westward movement 44–6
slave trade 36, 46, 133, 139; *126*
'Slavic legend' 44
Slavnikid dynasty 50, 98
Slovakia 123
Smolensk 148
'social Darwinism' 7
Sorbs 36, 45, 46, 64, 68
Spain 83, 84, 128, 133, 139
Stanislav, St 109; *109*
Stará Kourim, grave find *177*
Stara Zagora, relief *34*
Staré Město 179; *34*
*Stellerburg 32*
Stephen I of Hungary, St 51, 109, 183; *53*
Stettin, boat find 146; *147*
Strzelno abbey 194; *68, 195*
Styria 73, 149
Sudeten mts. 66
Suzdal region 132
Svatopluk 41, 49
Sviatoslav, prince 131
Swabia 157, 169
Sweden 12
Switzerland 158
Sylvester II, pope 99
Szigetszentimiklós-Háros grave find *34*

Tabor and Taborites 79, 122, 124; *80*
Tacitus 17–18, 22, 46
Tana 132–3
Tannenberg, battle of 11, 72, 149
Tatar invasion 61, 73, 84, 132
Teutonic knights 11, 55, 65, 67, 69, 70–2, 75, 110, 143; seat of the Grand Master *63*
textiles *see* cloth trade
Theodoric, Master 202; *76, 202*
Thomas of Štítný 116; *116*
Thorn (Toruń) 145, 148, 159; *145, 201*
Thorn, Treaty of 72
Tighina 133

timber trade 156–60; *159*
Tmutarakan 132
Töpfer, B. 114
Toruń *see* Thorn
towns *see* urban development
Toynbee, Arnold 8
trade 12, 36, 58, 60, 125–76 *passim*, 182, 184, 187, 191; *126, 127*
Transylvania 196, 198; mineral deposits 130
Trier 180
Trzebnica, nun's church *105*; Cistercian MS. *196*
Tuni, abbot 12, 180
Turks 78, 84, 109, 133

*Umlandfahrt* 150
universities, foundation of 77, 112, 203
urban development 60, 61, 111, 114, 117, 129, 144ff, 198
Urbánek, R. 121
Utraquists 122

Vagrians 64
Varangians 135, 178
Veit Stoss 199; *81, 199*
Venice 78, 129, 133, 149
Vienna 129
Vilzi 46
Vincent, Master 192
Vistula, R. 44
*Vita Beatissimi Stanislai* 198; *109*
Vitebsk 148
Vladimir region 132
Volga, R. 132, 138–9
Vratislav II 191
Vyšehrad Codex *96*

Wachok abbey, chapter house *105*
Waldemar Atterdag 111
Waldensian movement 115, 124
Waldhauser, Konrad 118
Wenceslaus, St 98, 109; *97*
Wenceslaus II 74; *75*
Wenceslaus III 74; *75*
Wenceslaus IV 121; *77, 113*
Wends 36, 64; crusade against 55, 65, 92, 143
Weser, R. 46, 144
Westphalia 144, 147, 169
Wilno, St Anne's *204*
wine 161–2, 166; *161*
Winrich of Kniprode 71, 111
Wisby 138
Wismar 146
Witelo 199
Wrocław *see* Breslau
Wycliffe and Wycliffites 119, 120, 124; *118*

Žižka, Jan 79, 122
Zsámbék, church at *105*